New Nations and Peoples

Morocco

Morocco

NEVILL BARBOUR

with 91 illustrations and 5 maps

New York
WALKER AND COMPANY

Library of Congress Catalog Card Number: 65-19258

First published in the United States of America in 1965 by Walker and Company, a division of Publications Development Corporation.

Printed in Great Britain

Contents

Preface

MOROCCO IS UNIQUE AMONG ARAB STATES in having a coast on the Atlantic as well as one on the Mediterranean. It is a country of great natural beauty. As a modern kingdom it has been independent only since 1956 and it has all the problems common to emergent states. But it also possesses something which most of them do not – a great history, stretching back more than a thousand years.

In 1189, when the domains of the Moroccan rulers extended from the Atlantic to Tunis and from the Sahara to the Tagus and the Ebro, the famous Saladin, wishing to besiege Acre, invited the participation of the Moroccan fleet. In 1211 King John of England sent an embassy to a later Moroccan ruler, with the object of safeguarding the possessions of the English Crown in Aquitaine in case a victorious Muslim army should cross the Pyrenees, as seemed possible at that moment. In the sixteenth century, Queen Elizabeth imported the sugar used in her palaces from Morocco, and toyed with the idea of accepting Moroccan financial and material aid in landing English troops in Portugal to support a pretender to the Portuguese throne or, later, in attacking the Spanish domains in America.

One result of this past is that Morocco, in addition to the variety of its landscape, has a number of medieval monuments which rival those of Spain as evidence of that former Muslim culture of the west which is commonly called Moorish.

Having a geographical position which enables her to avoid foreign complications by retiring within her own borders, Morocco made use of this means of self-protection during the eighteenth and nineteenth centuries. In consequence, she preserved her medieval form

7

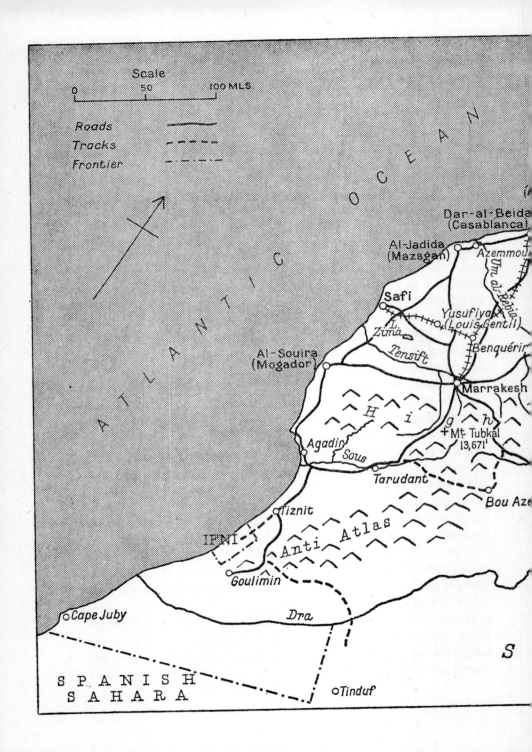

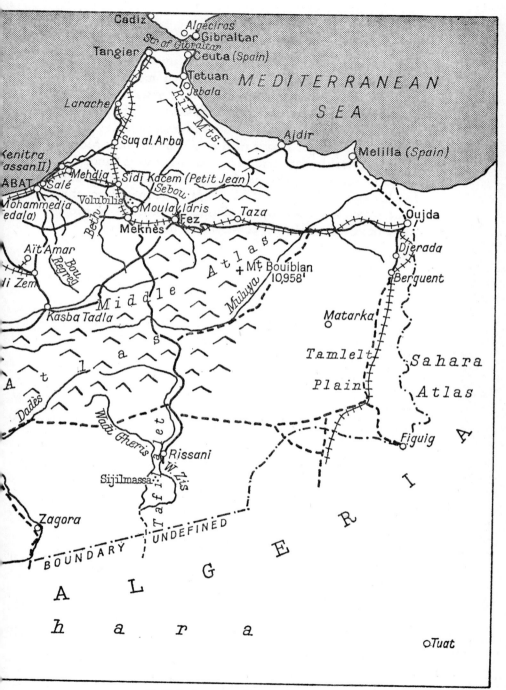

Political map of Morocco

of life until as late as the Franco-Spanish occupation of 1912. Her government and ways of life have since been modernized. The country today possesses a parliament of two houses of which the lower is elected by universal suffrage of both sexes. But the persistence of tradition adds the charm of contrast to Moroccan life.

In the following pages I have tried to picture the new Morocco against its historical background. The task is not easy. Since Great Britain in 1904 resigned to France her interest in Morocco's future, very few books have been written in England on the subject at all; and none which has attempted to illustrate Morocco's present by the past. I hope this work will contribute to that end.

1   Land and People

FOR MORE THAN EIGHT CENTURIES, from the time of
William the Conqueror to 1912, two Moroccan cities, Marrakesh
in the south and Fez in the north, held a pre-eminent position in that
country such as London and York at one time did in England.
The southern capital, Marrakesh, lies at the south-western limit of
the Moroccan coastal plain between the Atlantic and the Atlas.
The city is wide-spread, has low houses, and is more open and
African in character than other large Moroccan towns. To the north
it is bordered by a straggling palm grove; to the south by a vast
walled expanse of olive trees and orange orchards, known as the
Aguedal, a Berber word meaning an enclosed garden or pasturage.
If, on a clear winter or spring morning, you stand in the palm grove
to the north and look south across the city, you will see in the foreground red, crenellated walls. Above these there rises the magnificent, massive, square minaret of the Kutubia tower, built by an
Andalusian Muslim architect at the end of the twelfth century.
Beyond, in the distance some 50 miles away, you will see mile upon
mile of snow-clad mountains, rising at Mount Tubkal to nearly
14,000 feet.

Suppose you now travel some 200 to 250 miles north-east, either
through the plain or along the lower ranges of the Atlas, until you
reach the northern capital, Fez. Unlike Marrakesh, this is a city of
tall houses, covering the slopes on either side of the little river Fez,
with low mountains on the north, and the plateau of the Sais to the
south. If you stand beside the tombs of the Merinid Sultans, high
above the city among the olive groves, and look south-east, above
the walls and across the tangle of narrow streets and the green-tiled

sanctuary of Maulay Idris, you will see, 80 miles away, the majestic snow-covered mass of Mount Bouiblan, rising from the mountain ranges on either side of it to a height of over 10,000 feet.

The two peaks, Tubkal and Bouiblan, are summits at either end of the south-western section of the Atlas mountains, known in Berber as Adrar Deren. These rise on either side of the port of Agadir in south Morocco, coalesce and run north-east through the whole length of the country, bend eastwards to form the land-mass of Algeria, and finally fall to the level of the coastal plain some 50 miles short of the eastern shore of Tunisia. Morocco consists of 600 miles of the mountains between the Atlantic and Algeria and of the land on either side of them. The southern slopes, with the projection to the south which is known as the Anti-Atlas, end in the great Saharan desert; those on the north descend to the fertile Atlantic plain where the great majority of the Moroccan population live. It is the Atlas mountains, with the desert on the south and the Atlantic and the Mediterranean on the west and north, which give Morocco its variety of scenery and its extraordinary beauty. It is they that ensure the country a more plentiful water supply than other North African lands. It is from them that there emerge the rivers with the lovely names – on the side of the desert the Wadi Zis and the Wadi Gheris, which lose themselves in the wilderness after giving life to the oasis of Tafilalet; the Sous, which fertilizes the gardens around red-walled Tarudant; and the Dadès and the Todgha which flow down on the bare southern slopes of the Atlas, creating the green fertile valleys of Tineghir and Boulmane, shady with walnut and mulberry trees at the higher altitudes and with palm trees at the lower. Along them are strung out the strange waspnest-like walled villages or *ksur* of the Berbers and the towering *qasbas* or castles of their notables. From the northern slopes come other rivers – the Sebou, the Bou Regreg, and the Um al-Rebia which pour into the Atlantic; and the Muluya, which empties into the Mediterranean.

Lying at the extreme north-west of the African continent, Morocco differs from other Arab lands in possessing this coast-line on the Atlantic; it is no farther from America than are the most westerly lands of Europe. With territories to the south, known today as Mauritania (of which the present Spanish Sahara is geographically part), Morocco forms the most westerly portion of the Arab world and is therefore known to Arab geographers as al-Maghrib al-Aqsa or the Far West. During the Middle Ages, as in antiquity, the immensity of the Atlantic Ocean and its unsheltered Moroccan shores caused it to be regarded as an absolute barrier to the west. A modicum of trade was indeed carried on by sea with Europe, largely by Genoese and Venetians, but traffic with West Africa went by caravan across the desert. In the seventeenth century Muslim refugees from Spain made Rabat and Salé a centre of trade and privateering activities; by these they sought to gain a living and to revenge themselves on their Christian Spanish persecutors. It was however only after the construction of modern harbours at Casablanca and elsewhere, during the French protectorate in the first half of the present century, that traffic through the Atlantic ports acquired the importance in the country's life which it still retains today.

On the west the geographical limits of Morocco are clearly marked by the 700 miles of coast from Tangier to Cape Juby; they are made equally clear on the north by the 290 miles of coast on the Straits of Gibraltar and on the Mediterranean, from Tangier to the Algerian frontier. At one point however the distance across the Straits from the Moroccan coast to Tarifa in Spain is no more than 9 miles and there is in general no great difficulty in crossing from one shore to the other. Relations between the two countries have therefore often been intimate, sometimes friendly and sometimes hostile, and throughout history there has hardly ever been a moment at which some piece of territory on one shore has not been in possession of the government ruling on the other. Thus, from 1333 to 1411, when most of Spain was already again Christian, Gibraltar remained in Moroccan hands; and today we find Christian Spain in possession of two ports, Ceuta and Melilla, on the Moroccan shore, and of several small islands, the Chafarinas, the Peñon de Alhucemas, and Vélez de Gomara lying just off it. One can indeed regard the Iberian peninsula and Morocco, north of the Atlas, as forming a distinct region intermediate between Europe and Africa, Iberia being cut off from the rest of western Europe by the Pyrenees as Morocco is from the rest of Africa by the Atlas and the Sahara. For Morocco as a whole, however, the comparison is not entirely accurate since the Pyrenees simply mark the northern limit of Spain, while the Atlas, as we have seen, forms the backbone of Morocco.

While the shores of the Atlantic and the Mediterranean leave no doubt about the geographical frontiers of Morocco to the west and the north, the frontier as at present fixed is disputable in the south; and it is political rather than geographical in the east. South of the Atlas the desert stretches for a thousand miles. The inhabitants who live there are Muslims who derived their faith from Morocco; physically they resemble Moroccans rather than Negroes; like the majority of Moroccans they once spoke Berber but now speak Arabic. The dominant people in Mauritania consider themselves whites in contrast to the Negroes who become increasingly numerous towards the south. Until the French occupation after 1930 the whole area was known as the Moroccan Sahara, and is so described in the Franco-German exchange of letters after the Agadir crisis in 1911. It was the French government some thirty years ago who transferred the administration of the northern section from French-Moroccan to French-Algerian authorities and who later created the independent Islamic Republic of Mauritania farther south. This debatable area is limited to the north by the course of the river Dra and to the south by the Senegal and the bend of the Niger. From there the climate definitely changes. Such rain as falls occurs in the summer instead of in the winter and the population becomes exclusively Negro, while farther south we come to lands of tropical rainfall and primeval forest. The present frontier, which was imposed by the French and Spanish, runs south-west from Figuig on the Algerian border for some 400 miles and then, due west, along latitude 27·40 north. It thus excludes the whole of these disputed regions from Morocco.

On the east no abrupt transition marks the passage from Morocco to Algeria, either in the physical appearance or language of the people, or in the climate, or in the fauna and flora. The mountain ranges, the plateaux, and the valleys continue, and the same tribes

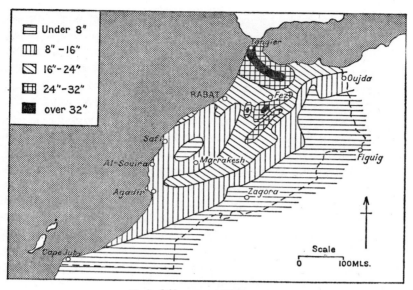

Rainfall map of Morocco

are found on either side of the frontier. The main line of communication by road and rail runs along the valley from Fez towards the
Moroccan frontier-town of Oujda through the Taza corridor, named
after the sleepy little city of Taza at the eastern end of the pass. North
of the corridor there lies a more or less isolated range of mountains,
known as the Jebala in the west and the Rif farther east. These
run parallel to the coast from Tangier nearly to Melilla and the more
easterly section, beginning at Targuist, constitutes the Rif properly so-
called. As in the Atlas the people here are Berber-speaking and it
was Ajdir, a mile or two inland from the little port of Alhucemas,
that the Rifi leader Mohammed Abdelkrim al-Khattabi made the
capital of his independent Republic of the Rif, during the epic
struggle first against the Spanish only, and then against the Spanish
and French, from 1921 to 1926. Except for the two ports of Ceuta
and Melilla, both in Spanish possession, and for Alhucemas, the
coast is for the most part precipitous and is little more hospitable
than the Atlantic. Geologically, northern Morocco is a detached
portion of Europe, and the Rif an extension of the Andalusian

Cordillera. Central Morocco is intermediary in age, while the far south belongs to an ancient primary continent. The area between Taza and the Algerian frontier forms the northern end of a vast semi-desert, pastoral plain, broken by an occasional river or oasis. This extends down the farther side of the Atlas from the mouth of the Muluya, as far south as Tafilalet, and then turns west to the estuary of the Dra; it is sometimes described as 'outer Morocco'.

The present frontiers represent the hard core of territory within which Morocco has existed as an independent state for a continuous period of nearly a thousand years, apart from the forty-four years interlude of the Franco-Spanish protectorate from 1912 to 1956. From this base Morocco has at times extended its authority as far afield as the Niger in the south, Tripoli in the east, and Saragossa in the north. On recovering independence in 1956, Morocco had the shape of an irregular quadrilateral. Its eastern and western frontiers are about 290 miles in length while the longer frontiers, running obliquely south-west and north-east, are about 700 miles. The sub-soil is fairly rich in minerals, particularly phosphates. Until the Portuguese expansion in the fifteenth to sixteenth centuries the Atlantic provided almost complete protection on the west. No invasion by Negroes from south of the Sahara is ever known to have been attempted. On the north, the Straits were not necessarily a barrier to peaceful or warlike relations with the peoples beyond them, but they were made so during the period of Moroccan weakness throughout the eighteenth and nineteenth centuries. The eastern frontier is mountainous and difficult, but there are possible lines of approach through the Taza corridor and along the plateaux farther south; and it was invasions from the east which gave Morocco its indigenous population, its religion, and its languages, with the exception of the French and Spanish contribution made under the protectorate during the last fifty years. Apart from classical antiquity, which is today as remote from the life of modern Morocco as it is from that of modern England, the cultural influences affecting Morocco, until the Franco-Spanish occupation, were thus exclusively Muslim, coming either from the east along the North African coast or from Muslim Spain to the north of the Straits.

Morocco, unlike the rest of the Arab world, was never subject to the Turks. Its cities were all Muslim foundations and given their distinctive character by Arab cultural influence as they developed in a Berber milieu. Today, apart from Spanish monuments such as the Mezquita at Cordoba and the Alhambra at Granada, Morocco contains the finest surviving examples of that western Muslim civilization, often called Moorish, which reached its highest development in Spain.

The census of 1960 stated the population of Morocco as 11,500,000. It included a minority of 300,000 Europeans, two-thirds of whom were French and one-third Spanish; their presence was due to the Franco-Spanish protectorate which lasted from 1912 to 1956. Most of them lived in the larger towns, though French settlers had developed large areas of modern agriculture and were still in possession of their properties in 1963.

There were also about 160,000 Jews. Having been settled in Morocco for centuries these can be considered as indigenous. Some, who are believed to have arrived in antiquity, call themselves Palestinians; others may be descendants of Berbers converted in Roman times; others are descendants of Jews expelled by the Christian rulers of Spain. As a result of the connexion with West Africa, and of the former use of Negroes as domestic slaves and as soldiers, there is a small minority who are black or of mixed descent as well as groups of dark-skinned people known as *haratin* who are cultivators in the oases, probably also of mixed origins.

The mass of the population however are *sunni* Muslims of the *Maliki* rite; the mother-tongue of the majority is Arabic or, in the case of about a third of the population, Berber. For purposes of writing, Arabic is used exclusively, except in so far as most members of the educated classes have received their instruction during the last fifty years mostly in French or Spanish. These are therefore perfectly at home in one or other of these languages, which also came to serve as the principal languages of administration at the higher levels. Arabs and Berbers resemble south Europeans physically and are indistinguishable from them in appearance when similarly dressed.

At the beginning of recorded history, the inhabitants of Morocco, as of the rest of North Africa, appear to have been Berber-speaking and of the white race. This population probably came from the Middle East, but we have no conclusive evidence of this and still less as to the date of their arrival. Before them there were prehistoric peoples who were responsible for the dolmens and tumuli which are found in various places, for example near Arzila. Some of these peoples lived in caves; and were the contemporaries of a tropical fauna of elephants, hippopotamuses, rhinoceroses, giraffes, and zebras. It is however with the Berber-speaking peoples that Moroccan history really begins. These were known in the east as Libyans, apparently a generic name for North Africans; as Numi-dians for those who lived in Tunisia and eastern Algeria; and as Mauri, for those who lived in western Algeria and Morocco. Mauri is the origin of the word 'Moor' whose use in modern times is very confusing. During the last century the term began to be used to describe the inhabitants of the territory known today as Mauritania; this lies hundreds of miles south of the Roman Mauritania to which the present Morocco corresponds. In the phrase 'the Moors in Spain', 'Moors' simply means western Muslims, of whom some only came from Morocco, as opposed to eastern Muslims or 'Saracens'. When reference is made to the 'Moors' of Ceylon or of the Philippines this does not imply any connexion with Morocco at all but simply indicates that the people concerned are Muslims. In the eighteenth century the English in India called Hindustani 'moorish', meaning the language of the Muslims of India.

No one racial type can be identified as Berber; the term is simply used conveniently for all those peoples who speak a dialect of a certain language which we call Berber. The language is not written and no standard form of it exists. Once spoken throughout North Africa, west of the Nile Valley, it still survives in the oasis of Siwa in the United Arab Republic and in small pockets in Tripolitania and Tunisia; in the west a form of it, known as Guanche, was spoken in the Canary Islands when these were colonized by the Spanish at the beginning of the fifteenth century. Today it is still widely spoken in Algeria where perhaps a million people use it,

principally in the Kabyle country and in the Aurès. In Morocco it is the mother-tongue of about 3,000,000 people, mostly in the High and Middle Atlas, in the Anti-Atlas, and in the Rif. The word 'Berber' itself is probably simply an adaptation of the Latin word *barbarus* which the Romans applied to populations talking languages other than Greek or Latin. Berbers refer to themselves as 'Imazighen' meaning the free or noble people and call their language 'Tamazight' or, in the south, 'Tashilhit'. Philologically Berber is held to be related on the one hand to the Semitic languages and on the other to languages of the Nile Valley such as ancient Egyptian.

The Berber-speaking groups are distinguished by their virility and love of independence. One remarkable fact about them is that the possession of a common language and of a common residence in a given area for over two thousand years appears never to have given them any conception of national unity in a political sense. The Numidian kingdoms of classical times under Massinissa and Jugurtha were Berber but seem to have adopted Punic civilization. In the Middle Ages the three great Berber dynasties of Morocco adopted the Arabic language for official purposes, and Arab systems of administration; and their leaders tried to establish genealogies to show that they were of Arab descent.

At the present time the Moroccans can be thought of as one people, having a sense of being Moroccans as opposed to Algerians or Tunisians. Certainly there are differences between the way of life of the Arab-speaking townsmen and the Berber-speaking peoples of the mountains. Under Berber customary law Berber women, for example, have fewer legal rights than Arab women under Islamic law, but they are freer in some practical respects such as the less frequent use of the veil. These differences however are variations between different categories of one society not symptoms of the conflict of two nationalities. There is, for example, no demand for education in the Berber language in Berber areas. The fact that the first Prime Minister of independent Morocco, Si Embarak Bekkai, was Berber had no more political significance than the fact that the British Prime Minister David Lloyd George during World War I was a Welshman.

Arabs and Berbers are alike proud of being Moroccans, and both regard Arabic as the language of religion, of administration, and of civilized intercourse in general. Moroccan newspapers, being written in Arabic, are as intelligible to Egyptians or to Syrians as their own newspapers are. This linguistic link with the rest of the Arab world implies a link of political sympathy in all matters of common interest to Arabs. Though Morocco has a very strongly marked individuality of its own, it is essentially a portion of the Arab world.

The eleven and a half million Moroccans are a young population; 51 per cent are less than twenty years old and 80 per cent than forty. The annual increase is nearly 3 per cent, a rate which, if maintained, would about double the population in a quarter of a century. Though 80 per cent of the people are rural, the considerable number of large and medium towns exert a powerful attraction on the inhabitants of outlying districts. The chief industrial centre, Casablanca, has all but a million inhabitants; the southern capital, Marrakesh, has a little over a quarter of a million, Fez a little under. Meknès has 171,000 inhabitants; Tangier 141,000; Oujda 127,000, and Tetuan 101,000.

All the larger cities lie to the north of the Atlas; to the south the largest, Tarudant, has a bare 15,000. The Jewish and Christian populations are 80 per cent urban; about one-third of all the Jews live in Casablanca. The two and a quarter million agricultural workers are virtually all Muslim, and so are the overwhelming majority of the 480,000 industrial workers, including those in mines and factories. There are some 25,000 teachers, while the police, army, and fire-services occupy 100,000 Moroccans.

The abruptness of the social transition which Morocco underwent between 1912, when it was still almost entirely medieval, and 1956 when it regained independence as a modern state has resulted in a great diversity in the aspect of the towns and in the way of life of the inhabitants. Until 1912 the gates of the walled cities were still closed at night and in many cases there were similar barriers dividing one quarter of the town from another. The contrast between life in the city and life outside was still as striking as it was in the England of the twelfth century. Like medieval kings elsewhere, the Sultan with his court until 1912 moved around his domains with an armed force, restoring order, living off the country, reducing unruly subjects, and collecting taxes. Difficulties of communication due to the absence of roads for wheeled traffic and of bridges over the rivers meant that each area and each city preserved a strongly marked individuality. Some little coastal towns, like Rabat or Mogador, are Andalusian in character, having low whitewashed houses, and planned rectangular streets. Marrakesh, already mentioned, has a more African aspect with its cheerful, crowded markets; in Fez the high houses with grey exteriors (like all medieval Muslim dwellings with few or no windows on to the street) is a self-centred, reserved, mysterious city. Its steeply sloping streets are so narrow that two animals can hardly pass and the bare walls give no indication of the handsome courtyards or spacious gardens which often lie behind them. The more open Meknès was a creation of Sultan Maulay Ismail at the end of the seventeenth and beginning of the eighteenth century; of the constructions produced by his passion for building there remain some monumental gateways and some vast arched buildings. Tetuan, Tangier, and Safi each have a picturesque quality of their own. Cities, such as Fez, Rabat, and Tetuan, which had contained a large element of population originating from Muslim Spain are regarded as *hadriya*, or cities of urban refinement in building, decorative, and culinary arts. On the establishment of the protectorate the first Resident General, Marshal Lyautey, decided to preserve the existing cities as far as possible, and to build modern towns outside the walls or even some distance away from the existing habitations. This has preserved Moroccan scenic beauty for the visitor; the result was however less appreciated by Moroccans who found themselves becoming living exhibits in cities, themselves museum pieces, where it became increasingly difficult to compete with the merchants and shopkeepers of the new sections which possessed facilities for modern transport. Those citizens who could do so began to move out to the new quarters or to the developing towns on the coast. Many of the beautiful Fez houses have thus been abandoned by owners who have moved to Casablanca or to the new administrative capital Rabat. As in Europe former residences are being used as orphanages, schools, political party headquarters, or for other utilitarian purposes. Some of the new houses in the old city now have exterior windows. The *suqs* or markets, once filled with the lovely products of local craftsmen, are now stocked with factory-made goods from Morocco itself or from abroad. Only a limited number of crafts, principally leather-work, pottery, and rugs, which can find a tourist market, are still flourishing today.

In the countryside the contrasts are equally striking. In such centres of colonization as exist around Meknès the modern orange farms and other forms of twentieth-century cultivation are run as efficiently as anywhere in the world. Elsewhere the methods of medieval subsistence agriculture still prevail. In general Berber cultivators live in solidly built houses, but there are also villages with houses of mud or of wattle, tent-dwellers, transhumants moving from summer to winter quarters, and nomads properly-speaking. South of the Atlas the majority live in the peculiar walled constructions known as *ksur*.

The *villes nouvelles* or new cities which have been erected since the protectorate are entirely modern in conception, with many buildings in the style known as neo-Moroccan. Casablanca contains some remarkable modern buildings of purely European style and others in which the native style has been successfully adapted.

Corresponding contrasts are to be seen in the clothing worn. The more conservative townsmen and the peasants in general have kept the traditional costume which was universal until 1912, but European clothes are increasingly the fashion. Women are still generally veiled in public though thousands of them are now working as teachers, nurses, or speakers on the radio, and it is already many years since the first Moroccan woman aviator took a pilot's licence. The contrast is piquant when a veiled lady is seen driving a powerful Cadillac or the veiled wife of an artisan goes riding on the carrier of her husband's motor-bicycle.

A large industrial proletariat exists in Casablanca, Fedala, Safi, and mining centres such as Khuribga. Since the last days of the protectorate the workers have been organized in powerful trades unions. Living standards however remain desperately low among unskilled workers of whom thousands live in deplorable *bidonvilles* or shanty towns that sprang up outside every large Moroccan city during the tremendous industrial and building boom after World War II. Efforts are being made to replace these bad living con-ditions by building simple, suitably designed houses, but the size of the problem and the industrial slump which followed independence means that the solution is not yet in sight.

1 The notable or chief of a Berber community lives, together with his family in large earth fortresses called *quasbas* (in Berber *tigremt*) such as this one at Skoura in Southern Morocco.

2 and 4 The two geographical features which isolate Morocco from the rest of Africa are the Atlas mountains (*left*) and the vast Sahara desert (*right*).

3 The Southern capital, Marrakesh, with its low houses is more African in character than other large Moroccan towns as this eighteenth-century drawing illustrates.

5 Rabat is typical of many Moroccan towns with its closely-packed houses. This is the Oudaia quarter of the town at the mouth of the river Bou Regreg.

6 'Berber' is a generic term which does not identify a particular racial group but applies to all who speak a 'Berber' dialect. This Berber man and boy are from the southern slopes of the Atlas Mountains.

7 In the old towns such as Fez animals are still the only means of transport for local craftsmen and merchants.

8 and 9   Berbers celebrate with traditional folk dancing, and these are typical dances of Southern Morocco.

10 As a result of Morocco's connexion with West Africa there is a small black or dark-skinned minority. This street musician is a member of the Gnawa Negro confraternity originally from West Africa.

11 This Jewish shoemaker is one of many thousands of Jews whose ancestors settled in Morocco either in antiquity or as a result of expulsion from Christian Spain.

12 New houses are replacing the shanty towns or *bidonvilles* which sprang up after the Second World War.

13 In the rural areas such as the Berber village of Ait Ben Haddu in Southern Morocco the traditional housing conditions still prevail.

14 The marriage feast is always associated with colour and festivity. This is a young bride at Rabat.

15 The charge of horsemen at the *fantasia* in the yearly celebration in honour of the early Muslim founder of the first Moroccan dynasty, Maulay Idris I.

2   Origins

MOROCCO ENTERS RECORDED HISTORY about 1100 B.C. when Phoenicians from Tyre in the Land of Canaan founded two trading posts or, as used to be said in English, 'factories' on the Atlantic coasts of Spain and Morocco a little beyond the Straits of Gibraltar. The colony on the Spanish coast was given the name Gadera (which later became Gades and finally Cadiz), meaning a fortified enclosure; while that on the Moroccan coast, named Liks, was situated by the mouth of the river Lukkus, close to the present⁄ day city of Larache. Close to each city, on promontories running into the sea, temples were built in honour of the Phoenician God Melqart, identified by the Greeks with Heracles and by the Latins with Hercules. The whole area of the Straits is in fact connected with the legend of Hercules. It was in the neighbourhood of Larache that there was believed to have existed the Garden of the Hesperides where grew the golden apples, guarded by the daughters of Atlas, which it was one of the labours of Hercules to fetch. Here too lived the evil giant Antaeus whose destructive career was ended in the course of the same labour. Either on this or some other occasion, the Hero was credited with having split open the Straits of Gibraltar, separating Africa from Europe.

Although we hardly have another glimpse of Morocco for some six hundred years after 1100 B.C. it is certain that a number of other 'factories' were during this time established in Morocco, either by the Phoenicians or by their former colony, the later independent state of Carthage. These posts lay on the route to Cadiz and Liks. They included Rusadir (in Punic 'the great headland'), today Melilla;

33

Tamuda, near Tetuan; Tingis, now Tangier; and Chella, across the river from the modern Salé. By preference such settlements were on isolated headlands, like Melilla, or on little islands just off the coast – the sort of sites familiar to Britishers at Gibraltar or Hong Kong. These cities were still minting coins with Punic inscriptions on them in the first century B.C. and from the emblems which they bear we can gather some idea of their products – bees and ears of wheat on the coins of Melilla; grapes and fish on those of Tingis; grapes and corn at Liks.

We can only conjecture how much influence these Punic settlements exerted beyond their immediate vicinity. The closest parallels are perhaps the European settlements on the west African coast a hundred and fifty years ago or European coastal settlements in China. It is important however to remember that Carthage was herself an African state; Carthaginians were not regarded by the Berbers as Europeans but more as the Arabs today are. There is no doubt that Carthage exerted great influence which lasted long after the destruction of the Carthaginian state in 146 B.C. The Romans probably worked through Punic-speaking officials in their relations with the Berbers just as French officials more recently did through Arabic-speaking officials. The Byzantine historian Procopius who accompanied Belisarius to North Africa in the seventh century A.D. says that Punic was still spoken at that time. The destruction of Carthage must have sent thousands of refugees to the Punic settlements in the west. In Morocco there are more traces of Punic inscriptions after the fall of Carthage than from before. Moreover there was another great centre of Carthaginian influence in Andalusia. No doubt waves of Semitic influence reached Morocco from across the Straits in Carthaginian times, just as they did later in the time of the Arabs.

From Roman sources we learn that Moroccan troops were serving with the Carthaginians in Sicily in 406 B.C. In the Second Punic War Moroccans were serving with the Carthaginians. In the Third Punic War, such aid was not forthcoming, though Carthaginian emissaries pointed out to the Mauritanian rulers that once Rome had mastered Carthage she would seek to extend her rule farther west.

From 200 B.C. it is clear that two Berber kingdoms existed in North Africa. One, which covered most of present-day Algeria, was known as Numidia; the other, Mauritania, coincided with the north-eastern portion of the present Kingdom of Morocco. The Berber rulers of these kingdoms had Carthaginian names and formed one related dynasty. The frontier dividing Numidia from Mauritania was normally the river Muluya; this enters the Mediterranean 15 miles west of the present Moroccan-Algerian frontier and under the protectorate it formed the eastern limit of the Spanish zone. The rulers of these states were inevitably involved in the civil dissensions of the Romans. In 106 B.C. Bocchus I, the ruler of Mauritania, first supported his son-in-law, Jugurtha, against the Romans and then, when his position became desperate betrayed him to them, rather as the Moroccan Sultan Abd al-Rahman was induced to deliver the Algerian leader Abd al-Quadir to the French, about 2,000 years later. In 82 B.C. the Roman general Sertorius, defeated in Spain, crossed to Africa and seized Tangier. After a few months, he returned to Spain, taking a body of Berber troops with him. The next mention of Tangier occurs when one of two joint Mauritanian rulers supported Antony while the other sided with Octavius, on whose behalf he organized a rising in Tangier against his brother. When Octavius emerged as victor, he rewarded Tangier by granting it in 38 B.C. the rights of a Roman city. In Algeria, King Juba I, who had supported Pompey, committed suicide after the Battle of Thapsus in 46 B.C. His kingdom was then placed under direct Roman administration and his son, also called Juba, after walking before Caesar's chariot during the latter's triumph, was given the best Graeco-Roman education available. In 30 B.C. it was the turn of Antony and Cleopatra to commit suicide. They left behind them their twin children, Alexander Helios (Sun) and Cleopatra Silene (Moon); these after having to walk in the triumph of Octavius were entrusted to Octavia, sister of Octavius and the widow of Mark Antony. Juba proved to be a studious and serious-minded prince and in 25 B.C. was made King of Mauritania; to this realm was added the whole of Numidia as far as Djidjelli. In this capacity he took the style of 'Juba II, King of the Mauritanians', or sometimes

'King of the Libyans', that is of the North Africans in general. To the west his authority probably ended at Rabat; in the east it extended to the Aurès while its limits were indeterminate in the south. Communications between the eastern and the western halves of the kingdom were by the Taza corridor or by sea. Within this kingdom Roman cities such as Tangier appear to have formed enclaves of Roman sovereignty. Arzila, for example, depended directly on the Roman authorities in Spain, having a status remarkably similar to that of Ceuta and Melilla at the time of the Spanish protectorate in the present century. On becoming King, Juba was affianced to Cleopatra Silene, now aged about eleven; the marriage probably took place in 19 B.C. when she was seventeen. This royal couple, Juba II and Cleopatra Silene, are the first Moroccan rulers about whom we have detailed information; their position was like that of recent rulers under the protectorate. Juba, as we have seen, was by origin an Algerian Berber with a background of Punic culture, as is evident from his name which is an abbreviation of Jubal meaning 'glory of Baal'. By his adoption into the Julian gens, Juba, whose official name was Caius Julius Juba, could claim descent from Venus. By his father he claimed descent from Hercules-Melqart through Tinga the wife, according to the legend, of Antaeus. After Hercules had slain her husband she was reputed to have borne the hero a son, named Syphax, who was considered to be the ancestor of the Numidian royal family. On the strength of this divine origin, Juba followed the example of his Roman patron and established his own worship as a god. As heir of the Ptolemies and the Pharaohs Queen Cleopatra Silene could claim even more exalted descent. A hoard of 7,000 of Juba's coins was found in Alcazarquivir in 1907; while these have his portrait with the inscription *Rex Juba* on the obverse they often have her portrait with the inscription *Basilissa Kleopatra* (and sometimes a crocodile) on the reverse. Other coins again bear her name without the King's; possibly she acted as regent for the three years during which he was away in Arabia gathering material for a book on that area.

Juba II, who reigned in all for forty-eight years, was described by a Roman historian as the 'most historically-minded of all kings'. In fact he wrote or compiled in Greek at least fifty works. Only a few quotations from them have survived but it is known that they dealt with history, geography, and a host of other matters. Apart from the account of Arabia, he wrote a description of the Canary Islands to which he sent an expedition; and he dedicated a whole brochure to a kind of spurge which he discovered in the Atlas. The milky juice of this he considered to have great merits in the treatment of conjunctivitis. The treatment became so popular that the Berber tribesmen who gathered the herb took to adulterating the juice with goat's milk to increase its apparent quantity. Juba also established a highly successful purple dye industry, probably at Mogador, utilizing a local shell fish. This became a great source of wealth. Juba was moreover a connoisseur of *objets d'art* and it is probably due to him that a number of exceptionally fine bronzes have been unearthed at Volubilis near the modern Meknès. This was probably his western, as Caesarea, today Cherchill, was his eastern, capital. His extensive library contained a number of Punic books.

Outwardly successful as Juba's reign was, he paid for his position as a Roman satellite with the unpleasantness of a succession of serious risings by his Numidian and Mauritanian compatriots and subjects. At the beginning of the Christian era a rising in southern Morocco and south-western Algeria lasted for over a decade. In A.D. 17 a fresh rising broke out in the Aurès near the modern Batna, in the precise neighbourhood where the Algerian rising against France in 1954 was to occur. But it was not till after Juba's death that a Roman victory (a little way inland from the modern Algiers) put an end to the rising and that King Ptolemy, Juba's son by Cleopatra, was allowed the insignia of triumph on his coinage, in A.D. 24.

After reigning for seventeen years, King Ptolemy was summoned by the half-mad Emperor Caligula to attend him during his visit to Lyon in A.D. 41. The two rulers were cousins, Ptolemy being grandson of Antony by Cleopatra and Caligula his great-grandson by Octavia. Entering the amphitheatre clad in one of the famous purple cloaks which had so much contributed to the royal wealth King Ptolemy was greeted by the crowd with an ovation. Furious with envy and covetousness, Caligula had the unfortunate monarch privately executed, without having brought any charge against him. Though Caligula was assassinated in the following year and Ptolemy was rehabilitated, as far at least as the writings of Roman historians went, his murder marked the final extinction of the Ptolemies and of the Mauritanian kingdom. The latter, now transformed into a Roman province, was divided by Caligula's successor Claudius into an eastern and a western portion, known as Mauritania Caesariensis and Mauritania Tingitanis respectively.

Reckless as Caligula's method had been, the annexation of Mauritania accorded with the Roman practice of using puppet kings only till such time as the Roman government felt it practicable to take direct control themselves. In this case however the out-rageous manner of the take-over provoked a rising which it took them 20,000 troops and three years to overcome. The leader of the revolt was a minister of the murdered King, by name Aedemon. It is characteristic of the persisting Punic and Berber climate of Mauri-tania that his father bore the Carthaginian name of Bostar (a contraction of Abd Astarte) while his mother came of Berber stock. After the rising had been suppressed locally the Roman commander led an expedition to the south across the Atlas as far as the river Guir and the modern Bou Denib. After the annexation the Roman governor still bore among his other designations the Punic title of *suffete* or judge.

It is probable that Tangier was the first capital of the Roman province but there is evidence that later Juba's capital, Volubilis, was the residence of the governor. The risings which had marked Juba's rule did not cease with the annexation. In the reign of Marcus Aurelius, during a rising which continued for five years, Mauri-tanians (Mauri) are reported to have crossed the Straits in the year 173 and to have overrun much of Spain. In 191 there was another rising in Volubilis; and there was further fighting between 253 and 268, which apparently originated in Numidia. Finally in 285 or a little later the Emperor Diocletian abandoned Volubilis and Salé, retaining only the triangle Larache-Tetuan-Tangier. This with the international zone of Tangier, corresponds exactly to the western section of the Spanish zone during the protectorate of 1912-56. It was attached to the Spanish 'dioceses', while Tangier itself apparently became the residence of the governor. The maintenance of this limited area of Roman sovereignty was no doubt considered necessary for the protection of traffic in the Straits; its attachment to Spain rather than to Mauritania Caesariensis was made necessary by the abandonment of the land connexion through the Taza corridor.

Mauritania Tingitanis seems always to have been something of a Cinderella among Roman provinces. We have little knowledge of it at all and know of no distinguished persons who originated in it. Archaeological research has revealed few notable remains apart from those at Volubilis near the modern Meknès. This does not of course prove that there may not have been other notable cities; but the fact that no trace has been found of paved Roman roads such as exist in Algeria and Tunisia indicates that the province was relatively undeveloped. We know that the main lines of communication ran from Tangier to Salé, with a deviation in the neighbourhood of Liks leading to Volubilis, but these were probably what the French call *pistes* or tracks intended primarily for pack animals. In the earlier stage of Mauritania we can perhaps think of the protected kingdom as bearing the same sort of relationship to more developed provinces as Nepal, with its Gurkha mercenaries, did to British India. Under Juba II there was clearly a brilliant and sophisticated court, which we should today describe as Levantine, and its base a backward and discontented people. This background persisted under direct Roman administration. Christianity seems to have penetrated the country fairly extensively by the middle of the third century and there were at least four bishoprics in western Mauritania. We hear also of a local Christian martyr at Tangier named Cassian immediately before Constantine's adoption of Christianity. The governor in Roman times had the rank of procurator prolegate; the garrison seems normally not to have exceeded 14,000 men. The southern frontier was a little to the south of Salé.

After Diocletian's withdrawal, the obscurity is even completer. A hundred and fifty years later, the Vandal king Genseric transported his 80,000 followers by sea from Tarifa to Morocco, probably landing at Ceuta. The Vandals then marched east in a body, possibly leaving a garrison in Ceuta. In the treaty which Genseric made with the Byzantine Emperor in 422, there is no mention of any territory west of the Muluya. When Justinian regained eastern North Africa in 535, the only portion of Morocco which he occupied was Ceuta, where he built a fortress and dedicated a church to the Virgin.

Nevertheless archaeological evidence, principally at Volubilis, shows that enough romanized Mauritanians remained to carry on some sort of Roman life for a whole 300 years after Diocletian's withdrawal. This conclusion is to be drawn from Latin inscriptions which date from between 599 and 635 and refer to officials holding such titles as *princeps* and *vice-propositus*. The non-Roman local origins of this population are revealed by names like Julius Matif, Julius Nuffusi, and Julius Mirzil. These personages seem to have belonged to the people known as the Baquates who played a great part in the affairs of the Volubilis area as early as the time of Diocletian.

Whatever the extent of Roman survivals may have been, it was the coming of the Arabs at the end of the seventh century A.D. which gave Morocco the character which it has ever since possessed. It made the country a portion of the Arab world which differed from other Arab territories mainly because of the importance of the Berber background. For the moment it served principally as the channel through which the nascent Islamic civilization passed into Spain. It was only when the splendour of Andalusian Islam began to decay, and the highly civilized Muslims of Spain began to pass over into Morocco, some as refugees from civil strife in Anda-lusia, some brought over as employees of the Moroccan government, and some as refugees from the Christian reconquest, that Morocco acquired its later position as the leading representative of Islamic civilization in the west.

As the writing of history was not developed by the Arabs until much later, and Morocco was remote from the existing centres of civilization, we have little reliable information concerning the means by which Arab rule and the religion of Islam were established in the west. We have to deduce the nature of the process from the results which it produced. Unlike the Roman conquest, the coming of

Islam did not immediately result in an impressive material development but brought about a rapid amalgamation of Arab and Berber
elements and so produced a new type of society. This society had its
periods of splendour and of decay, but was so natural to the country
that it has persisted from that day to this.

The few details which we know of the conquest and of the spread
of Islam in Morocco show that the first Arab raiding parties reached
Tripolitania about A.D. 647, some twenty-five years after the emigra-
tion of the Prophet Muhammad from Mecca to Medina. By 670 an
Arab governor, Uqba ibn Nafi, had founded the city of Kairawan
and was in control of southern and central Tunisia. When Uqba
was superseded in 674, his successor made a raid along the coastal
regions as far as Tlemsen near the present Moroccan border. Reappointed governor about 680, Uqba himself made a second raid
to the far west. Instead of keeping near the coast, however, he moved
westward, north of the Aurès, passed Tahert (the site of the modern
Tiaret) in south-western Algeria, and then moved north to Ceuta
by a route which has not been recorded. The governor of this city,
known as Count Julian, was probably a local leader whose position
as governor had been confirmed by the Byzantine Emperor. He came
to terms with Uqba, was confirmed in his post in the name of the
Caliph at Damascus, and the city was not molested. Tangier on the
contrary, which seems to have been in the possession of Berber
tribesmen, resisted Uqba, who thereupon captured it, massacred the
defenders, and took many slaves. Advancing inland, he reached
Volubilis and thence proceeded along the Middle Atlas to the plain
near where Marrakesh now stands. Here he captured the city of Nafis,
near the later city of Aghmat. It is said to have been defended by
roum (Byzantines); this might mean Christians or simply Romanized
Mauritanians. Advancing south into the Sous beyond Agadir, he
came across the Sanhaja Berbers, men who like the modern Tuaregs
wore a muffler over their mouths and were to found one of the
greatest Moroccan dynasties, 300 years later. Reaching the Atlantic,
Uqba is said to have ridden his horse into the ocean until the water
came up to its neck and then cried aloud, 'O God, I take you to
witness that there is no ford here. If there were, I would cross.' He

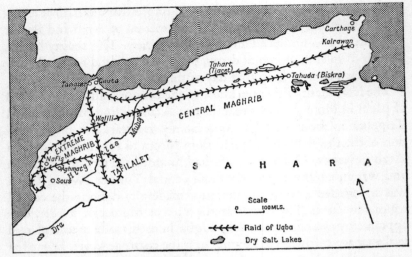

The Raid of Uqba *c.* 680

then returned eastward. On reaching the neighbourhood of Biskra he was intercepted, suffered a complete defeat, and was killed. The expedition, if the account is to be accepted, must have made its way through some 3,000 miles of totally unfamiliar country. We can only guess how far Uqba's raid brought any part of Morocco under lasting Arab control; but according to Arab historians a great many Berbers were converted to Islam. We do know that within thirty-one years, another Arab governor, Musa ibn Nusair, had established Arab rule in northern Morocco so firmly that he could use Tangier as a base for the Arab invasion and conquest of Spain. While the imposition of Arab rule in Ifriqiya (that is Tunisia) involved heavy fighting for a prolonged period, Morocco seems to have been assimilated much more easily.

The obscurity is heightened by the fact that we do not know in what proportions the country was Christian, Jewish, or pagan at the moment of the conquest. There certainly must have been Christians at the coming of the Arabs. This is shown by the inscriptions from Volubilis and is suggested by a number of references by Arab historians, such as the story that there was a Christian hermit living in the neighbourhood of Fez at the time of its foundation between 780 and 830 and the fact that the gates of the original city included a Bab al-Kanisa which presumably means 'the Gate of the Church'. The Jews of Morocco survived and have always been a numerous element in the country and it is not known how the Christians came to disappear from Morocco. In the Middle East and in Spain they were well treated by the early Muslims and remained a large and important element of the population. The only deduction which seems possible is that Christianity was associated in North Africa with Roman civilization, that it never became thoroughly indigenous, and in consequence withered away when the foreign rule which introduced it was removed.

Granting this, we still have to explain the apparently very rapid spread of Islam and of the use of the Arabic language. A number of factors no doubt contributed to produce this result. In the first place we must put the military prowess of the Arabs in their sudden eruption from Arabia. In the second place we have to take into account the magnetic effect of the intense faith which animated large numbers of the invaders, leaders and men alike, however many others of them may also have been influenced by the love of glory or of booty. In the third place there is the Quran, delivered to the Prophet in Arabic and so giving a quality of sanctity to the Arabic language. In the fourth place is the extraordinary power possessed by the Arabs of assimilating other peoples to themselves, at least when they are of kindred Semitic or similar culture. In the fifth place we must assume a certain affinity of spirit between Berber and Arab which had not existed between Berber and Roman.

In general the Arab conquest of North Africa resembled the Spanish conquest of central and southern America rather than the military and trading conquests of the English and the French in more recent times. In the case of the Arabs as in that of the Spanish intense devotion to the propagation of their faith was mingled with ruthless assertion of their military superiority. Just as the Spanish carried out mass conversions of American Indians to Christianity, by sprinkling an assembled multitude with Holy Water, declaring

them Christians by this baptism, and then leaving it to later instruction to perfect their knowledge of their new religion, so it is possible
to think of the mass conversion of the Berbers by the recital of the
shahada or declaration of faith and their gradual subsequent instruction in the articles and practice of their new religion. An Arab
historian makes the statement that there was at one moment a force
of 17,000 Arabs and 12,000 Berbers in Tangier and that it was
regarded as one of the duties of the Arab soldiers to instruct their
Berber companions in the practice of their religion. When the Arab
troops were later withdrawn we learn that a special body of thirty-
seven selected Arabs were attached to the Berbers as instructors in
religion. Presumably the process was soon completed by the education of the children in Quranic schools, known in Moroccan
dialect as *msid*, a corruption of the word *masjid*, a mosque. We know
also that in 718 the pious Caliph Omar ibn Abdelaziz sent a letter
urging the conversion of the Berbers. At the same time he despatched
a group of doctors of the law and forbade the drinking of wine.

Characteristic of the readiness with which the Arabs assimilated
newly converted peoples is the fact that the Arab conquest of Spain
was brought about, in 711, by a force which was largely Berber in
composition, hardly more than thirty years after the first appearance
of the Arabs in Morocco. It was commanded by Tariq ibn Ziyad
who was himself in all probability a Berber and certainly not an
Arab. Since the conquest was definitely an Arab not a Moroccan
operation, being approved from Damascus and executed by the
instructions of the Arab viceroy in Kairawan, this is a remarkable
tribute to the degree which assimilation had already reached. It can
be contrasted with the position in Algeria in modern times. After
125 years of French rule, no native Algerian had reached a high rank
in the army and no Algerian official had attained the position of
prefect or of judge in his own country, let alone been in a position
to play an outstanding part in French history. Since there are
singularly few traces of Berber influence to be found in Spain, even
in place-names or words adopted into Spanish, it is to be supposed
that those Berbers who settled there were already to an appreciable
extent arabized.

For some thirty years after the invasion of Spain, Morocco remained a province of the Arab Caliphate, governed by a deputy of the Arab viceroy in Kairawan. The viceroys enjoyed a great deal of independence of Damascus, until such moment as they were recalled; and their deputies in the remote Morocco were in the same position with regard to themselves. Once again we are reminded of the parallel with the Spanish *conquistadores* in America. Here the comparison is in favour of the Spanish régime, for the Spanish monarchy retained control of its distant dominions for three centuries, although they were separated by the ocean from the seat of government, while the Arab Caliphs lost all control within a quarter of a century. The cause is not difficult to see. Before the Spanish monarchy embarked on imperial expansion it had been consolidated by centuries of struggle, while the Christian faith in the west had also evolved a stabilized and universally recognized form long before it was transplanted to America. Islam on the contrary was from the very beginning intimately associated with a rapidly expanding empire and it reached Morocco before the conflict with the early heresies had been resolved in favour of a generally accepted orthodoxy. When the Caliphate itself became a subject of dissension, with the failure of the Alids to retain it, and the Umayyad dynasty in its turn was overthrown by the Abbasids the way was opened for members of the defeated parties to establish positions for themselves in the outlying provinces, in some cases as heads of some heretical sect. In this way for example an heretical kingdom was established at Sijilmassa, in the pre-Saharan region of south-east Morocco. The authority of the Caliphs was shaken in 739 when a governor named al-Muradi led an expedition into the Sous where he collected a rich booty. This operation roused alarm in other parts of Morocco and in 740 a revolt broke out, headed by a former water-carrier from Algeria by name Maisara. He succeeded in capturing Tangier and in murdering al-Muradi. He then proposed to set himself up as Caliph in the Atlantic plain. His own rule however was more tyrannical than that of the governor whom he had assassinated and in consequence he was soon defeated by troops from the east. In 742 a Berber, with the Arab name Salih, proclaimed himself prophet in the same area, producing a Berber sacred book, obviously suggested by the Quran. The distorted Berber version of Islam, which he established, with himself as prophet, had a considerable success and was accepted by the important tribe the Barghawata who occupied the southern coastal plain. It remained the recognized faith of a Berber kingdom, established by the Barghawata, which lasted for some 300 years. The area seems at this period to have been purely Berber and thickly populated with villages.

Long-lived as the Barghawata religion proved, it ultimately passed away without leaving a trace. The seed of the future Kingdom of Morocco was, on the contrary, sown in the year 788 when a refugee of the family of Ali arrived in Morocco after a dangerous journey, escorted by a faithful retainer named Rashid. After visiting Tangier the travellers made their way to Volubilis where they were well received by the local Auruba tribe. These were, in the Berber way, deeply impressed by the sanctity attaching to Idris as great-grandson of the Prophet. Thanks to his personal merits, to the wise advice of his henchman, and to the respect which Berbers have for those personages reputed to possess *baraka*, that is the charismatic power of emitting blessing and producing well-being, Idris was accepted as the leader and Imam of a coalition of Berber tribes. In Alid circles, the position of Imam implied civil and military leadership as well as religious. Once established, Idris began a series of attacks on neigh-bouring areas; these seem to have been directed to inducing Christians, Jews, and pagans to acknowledge Muslim overlordship. He seems not to have come into conflict with either the heretical Muslims of Sijilmassa or with the Barghawata south of the modern Casablanca. His successes were however sufficient to alarm the Abbasid ruler, Harun al-Rashid; the latter therefore despatched an emissary to win the confidence of Idris in order to poison him. This he was successful in doing.

Idris left no son, but a Berber wife bore him a posthumous child who was accepted as his successor, first under the regency of Rashid and then of another Arab. In 808, at the age of seventeen, Idris II took over control himself.

His position as Arab ruler was strengthened from time to time by the arrival of other Arabs. He had an Arab as chief minister and 500 more as a bodyguard. The significance of his reign is that it established in a rudimentary form the type of Moroccan kingdom which has existed ever since. This is a Muslim administration of which the methods are Arab, the official language is Arabic, and Arab arts and literature are encouraged. In this way Morocco was set on the path of becoming, by gentle and almost imperceptible stages, Muslim and Arabic-speaking. Not that the Arabs ever proclaimed that Morocco was Arab in the way that the French were later to proclaim that Algeria was French. On the contrary, the Berber-speaking basis of the country was always recognized, and newly assimilated Berber areas for a time retained their customary law. Nevertheless, as the country became increasingly Muslim, the fact that the Quran was delivered in Arabic and that Islam arrived from the Arab east had the effect of emphasizing the Arab element in Morocco rather as the practice of the Catholicism of Rome inevitably promotes a certain degree of the Latin outlook and civilization. Perhaps the greatest material achievement of Idris II in this respect was making Fez his capital. Coins have indeed been found which were minted in Fez already in 801, long before the foundation by Idris II. This settlement however was probably a primitive Berber agglomeration, on the right bank of the Wadi Fez, where the Andalus quarter is now situated. It is Idris II whom tradition credits with founding the city and it was in fact he who made it the capital, creating on the left bank of the river what was for over 200 years a separate city, where he built a palace called Al-Aliya in the district known today as the Qarawiyin quarter. The site was admirably chosen. Situated in the heart of fertile northern Morocco, Fez lies on the route from the Atlantic to the east through Taza at the point where it is crossed by the north–south route leading through the Atlas from the Rif and from Tangier to Tafilalet. The surrounding area is fertile and the city supplied with abundance of water. In 818 the urban character of the inhabitants was enhanced by the arrival of several thousand refugees who had been expelled from Cordoba; in 825 they were joined by another large group who came from Kairawan, the most advanced centre of Arab civilization in the eastern Maghrib as Cordoba was in the west. In consequence Fez became a centre from which Arab and Islamic influences radiated throughout northern Morocco. After Idris II's death the process was carried on by the formation of a number of little Idrisid kingdoms run on similar principles. Three of these were in the north between Tangier and Oran; one was on the borders of the Middle Atlas, while yet another was established in the far south, near the present Spanish enclave of Ifni.

It has however to be noted that the civilization of Fez like that of most medieval cities was highly self-centred. The city life was concentrated within the walls and there was little confidence between the citizens of the town and the cultivators outside who had a totally different form of life. In this respect Fez recalls Carthage – a rich trading centre, a city of merchant princes, leading a life in some ways highly refined, with a strongly developed religious and artistic sense. The citizens had contacts with their likes in other cities and abroad – in modern times with Manchester before the French protectorate and with Lyons during it – and were yet in a sense confined to their own precincts rather as the Europeans were in the former treaty ports of China or in Hong Kong today.

We can thus picture the ninth century as a time when Islamic and Arab influences began to irradiate the surrounding Berber environment from a number of centres like Fez and the other Idrisid capitals. In the plain south of Casablanca the Barghawata state by its adoption of a Berber distortion of Islam paid its own tribute to the influence of that faith even while it rejected it. Bordering the Mediterranean, we find three other tiny states; one near Tetuan, also with a religion of its own founded by a Berber prophet, and two others, one near Ceuta and the other near Alhucemas, both of which seem to have been more or less orthodox Muslim.

3 The Almoravid Empire

THE ASSASSINATION of Idris I by order of Harun al-Rashid was the last effective intervention of the eastern Caliphs in Morocco. From 790 for over a hundred years Morocco was affected by events in the greater Arab world only in so far as they caused the settlement in Fez of the two groups of refugees already mentioned. In the tenth century the position changed completely. By now two great Muslim kingdoms had come into being; the Amirate (later Caliphate) of Cordoba, and the heretical *Shia* Caliphate of the Fatimids in Tunisia. The latter naturally sought to spread their own type of religion, and with it their rule, into the western Maghrib. In 917 the Fatimids put an end to the little state at Alhucemas and in 922 they imposed their supremacy on the Idrisid ruler, Yahya IV. As *Shia*, the Fatimids were by nature hostile to the *sunni* régime in Cordoba and their advance was felt there as a menace. In 929 the Caliph Abder-rahman III of Cordoba, to avert this menace, captured Melilla, Ceuta, and Tangier. When however the Fatimids in 969 conquered Egypt and removed the seat of their government to their newly founded capital of Cairo, they lost interest in the Far West and by degrees their authority lapsed even in Tunisia. For the moment this left the field free to Spanish influences but sixty years later, in 1031, the sudden collapse of the Cordoba Caliphate freed Morocco from any likelihood of domination from Spain. As a result the ground was cleared for the emergence of a great Moroccan dynasty. This first brought the whole of Morocco under one central authority, next extended its rule over the Maghrib as far as Algiers, and eventually over the whole of Muslim Spain.

This achievement was the work of the Almoravids. These were

Berber-speaking nomads, known as the Sanhaja. They lived in what is today known as Mauritania and have given their name to Senegal. They were camel-breeders and their clothing was of wool. They ate camel's flesh and drank camel's milk; bread formed no part of their ordinary diet, the cultivation of the soil being virtually unknown to them. They had the striking habit of covering their mouths with a muffler or veil, known as a *litham*, for which reason they are known in Arabic as *al-mulaththamun* or veiled men. The practice still exists today among the Tuaregs of southern Algeria who are the most typical surviving nomadic Berbers. In about 1050 a pious Sanhajan prince made the pilgrimage to Mecca; in consequence of his journey he realized his own people's ignorance of the religion which they professed and was shocked at it. He therefore sought for a missionary who would instruct them. After several unsuccessful attempts, he secured the services of a pious Moroccan *faqih* or practitioner of religious law, by name Abdullah Yasin, who was a native of the Sous. Yasin was not a man of any particular theological learning but a simple-minded puritan. He began his mission by attacking practices forbidden by Islam, such as the drinking of wine, the taking of more than four wives, and indulgence in music – this art being associated amongst the nomads with singing, girls, wine, and fornication. His puritanism provoked such a violent reaction that he thought of abandoning his mission. Encouraged however by some of the principal men, he retired with them to an island, either in the Senegal or the Niger or off the coast of Mauritania. Here he founded a fortified monastery or *ribát* and concentrated in it a combatant religious community. The members were subjected to a fierce discipline; those who were detected drinking wine or lying were awarded eighty lashes; those who failed to prostrate themselves properly at prayer, twenty; and those who were late for prayer, five.

When a sufficient number of these monastic warriors had been collected, they began to sally forth and forcibly impose their form of religion upon others. The military operations were directed by one of the early adepts named Yahya ibn Umar while Abdullah Yasin retained religious and general control.

The first state to collapse under this assault was the *Shia* community at Sijilmassa. The primitive little capital was sacked; the 'places of pleasure' (presumably cabarets) were suppressed and the instruments of music destroyed. In 1054 a similar fate overtook the towns of Audaghost and Tagant in the black kingdom of Ghana in the south of the Sahara. On the death of Yahya he was succeeded by his brother Abu Bakr. In 1056 the latter captured Tarudant in the Sous, destroying there another little *Shia* state, which had been founded as a result of Fatimid influence. He then passed to the north of the Atlas, capturing Aghmat (which had replaced the earlier city of Nafis, captured by Uqba). Here he married the widow of the former ruler, a beautiful and intelligent Berber woman named Zeinab. Three years later Ibn Yasin was killed in an attack on the Barghawata in the coastal plain, but in subsequent fighting the heretical power was virtually destroyed by Abu Bakr. Receiving news of dissensions among the Sanhaja in the Sahara in 1061 the latter returned to the south, leaving his cousin Yusuf ibn Tashfin in charge in Morocco. At the same time he divorced Zeinab so that she could marry Yusuf, saying that she was too delicate a person to be exposed to the heat of the Sahara. The decision was epoch-making, since Yusuf was destined to unite Morocco and to extend Sanhaja authority over Muslim Spain and most of the Maghrib.

In 1062 Yusuf, left to himself, founded a fortified camp at Marrakesh which was soon to develop into a capital city. For the moment it was rather a base from which he could keep a watch on the settled Berbers, known as Masmouda, who lived in the Atlas and were traditionally hostile to the nomads from the south. The Almoravids could not count on the loyalty of the inhabitants of Aghmat, while its position among olive groves in the foothills did not in any case appeal to nomads who prefer open spaces and distrust wooded country.

Like the Umayyad prince who founded the Amirate of Cordoba, the Almoravids seem to have felt a nostalgia for the palm trees of their youth. By an ingenious application of the use of the *khattara* or artificial underground water channels, used to irrigate the Sahara oases, they brought water from the foothills to support the palm grove which is still a feature of Marrakesh. Besides preparing the way for the construction of a capital, Yusuf organized his Saharans into a disciplined force and set up the rudiments of an administration, appointing governors for the various regions which he controlled. When Abu Bakr in due course returned from the south, he found Yusuf and Zeinab so firmly established that he thought it best to accept the gifts which Yusuf, at Zeinab's suggestion, offered him so that (as they told him) 'he might lack for nothing in the desert'. He then withdrew to his desert realm, and left Morocco to Yusuf as an independent kingdom.

From 1062 to 1069, while William the Conqueror and the Normans were establishing themselves in England, Yusuf was completing the conquest of northern Morocco. Fez was taken for the first time in 1063 and again, this time definitely, in 1069. Once established in the north, the Almoravids were brought into contact with Andalusian Muslims and their methods. An Arab historian wrote about this time:

North Africa may be said to have derived its present wealth and important commerce from Spanish Muslims settling in it. When God was pleased to afflict Spain with the recent disastrous civil war (following on the fall of the Caliphate), thousands of Muslims of all classes and professions arrived on these shores. . . . Agriculture was developed by newly arrived farmers, springs were discovered and used for irrigation; trees were planted; watermills and other useful machinery constructed.[1]

Impressed by the possibilities of Fez, Yusuf made use of Andalusian talent to improve the city by joining the two separate towns into one and to endow it with new mosques, baths, *fonduks* (a combination of inn and warehouse), and mills; and he enlarged and improved the market. At the top of the town a fort was built at Bu Jeloud to serve as residence for the governor. By now, too, ingenious use was already made of the river to supply the houses with running water. 'In the Qarawiyin quarter', wrote the geographer, al-Bakri, who died in 1094, 'every householder has his own mill outside his door, his own garden with a variety of fruit trees, and running water passing through his house.' The Andalusian Muslims were no doubt equally valuable in organizing the machinery of government, while commerce was promoted by the presence of a large Jewish community. In 1075 Yusuf gained control of Taza and by 1082 held Melilla, Tlemsen, Oran, and all the country to Algiers.

Meanwhile, the collapse of the Caliphate of Cordoba resulted in the division of Muslim Spain into no less than twenty-six tiny states. These modelled themselves on the Caliphate without the means to support their pretensions. A contemporary eastern Arab poet wrote: 'In al-Andalus I cannot stomach the al-Muqtadirs and al-Muatamids. They inflate themselves with these misplaced titles of the Caliphs, like cats that swell themselves up to look like lions!'[2]

Almost overnight the Muslims, from dominating the peninsula, found themselves threatened with complete subjection to the Christian states of northern Spain. In their distress the rulers of the little states began to think of appealing for aid to their less civilized but more virile co-religionists south of the Straits. In 1085, the loss of Toledo to the Christians was a warning which could not be ignored. King Alfonso, who was already styling himself 'King of the men of the Two Religions', was now in a position to extort 'protection' money from the strongest of the Muslim states.

Even so, it was not without much hesitation that the ruler of the most active of the little kingdoms, King Muatamid of Seville, equally famous as soldier and as poet, brought himself to invoke the aid of the Africans. The latter were regarded by the Andalusians as only just emerging from barbarism. Finally al-Muatamid overruled the objections of his son and heir, saying that he 'did not wish his name to be remembered for evil in all the pulpits of al-Andalus'. 'For my part', he said, 'I prefer to be a camel-herd in Africa rather than a swine-herd in Castile.' After the fall of Toledo he sent an urgent request for help to Yusuf.

The latter was by now a man of seventy. He is described as of moderate height and slim, having a brown skin with little hair on his face. He had black eyes, an aquiline nose, curly hair, with a lock reaching down to his ears. His voice was soft. In his clothing and food he retained the simplicity of his desert forbears even after he had become ruler of a great empire. Always ready to attend to the needs of his subjects, his presence inspired respect and his justice was as well known as his courage. A man of sincere piety, as well as a shrewd and capable ruler, he typified all that was best in the Almoravid system. It was a puritanical movement; as it had no theological theories peculiar to itself it simply adopted the Muslim rite which was already in local use, namely the *Maliki*. Even at the height of his power Yusuf never sought to assume the title of *Amir al-Muminin* (Commander of the Faithful) but contented himself with that of *Amir al-Muslimin* (Commander of the Muslims) which denoted his imperial stature without implying a claim to the rank of Caliph as the title *Amir al-Muminin* would have done.

For a ruler of his age, character, and caution, the invitation to conduct a Holy War in Spain was not a matter to be accepted lightly. When he was first asked, he replied that he could not consider doing so until the ports on the Moroccan shore of the Straits were in his possession. When they were, he stipulated that he must have a port under his direct control on the Spanish shore also and bargained for Algeciras. While he had had wide experience of fighting in North Africa, he knew nothing of fighting against Christians. Equally important was the question of his relations with his fellow Muslims in al-Andalus. The Muslim Spain of the eleventh century was a very different place from contemporary Morocco. It was the home of a highly sophisticated and cultured but pleasure-loving and often corrupt Muslim society, in which Yusuf was not at all likely to feel at ease. Indeed, in some respects Almoravid society was more like that of the vigorous but rough Christian kingdoms of the north than that of Muslim Spain. Yusuf for example, might very well, one feels, have used to the Muslims of Seville precisely the language which a Muslim historian attributes to Yusuf's contemporary the Christian hero, Ruy Diaz the Cid, when he captured Valencia. The Cid is recorded as saying:

I have decided to judge your affairs on two days each week, on Mondays and Fridays; but if you have urgent cases, come to me on whatever day you like and I will hear them. I shall not be spending my time privately in the company of women, with wine and song, as your lords are accustomed to do, with the result that you cannot approach them when you have need of them.[3]

Yusuf seems indeed to have been as reluctant to accept al-Muatamid's

54

request as the latter was to make it. On the other hand the King of Seville was the Muslim prince of Spain for whom Yusuf was most likely to feel a measure of sympathy. For al-Muatamid, though notorious for his love of luxury and his taste for wine, was also a soldier of courage and resolution, while the fact that he had taken the lead in inviting Yusuf showed that in the last resort Muslim sentiment prevailed in him over any feeling that he might have for the Christian princes as fellow Spaniards. In 1086 therefore Yusuf crossed the Straits and after establishing a base at Algeciras advanced with his Andalusian allies towards Badajoz. Here the Castilian king, Alfonso, forced to abandon the siege of Muslim Saragossa, came to meet him. In the Battle of Zallaqa, or in Spanish *Sagrajas*, fought on 23 October 1086 Yusuf's forces with the aid of the Sevillans who alone of the Andalusian allies fought with distinction (al-Muatamid received more than one wound) won a resounding victory. Yusuf made no attempt to follow up this success; probably he had never had the intention of doing more than restoring the Muslim position and then leaving it to the Spanish Muslims to look after themselves. No doubt he was also affected by the news that his eldest son and prospective heir had died in Ceuta during his absence. Whatever his motives were, he returned to Morocco immediately, leaving 3,000 troops in Spain to assist the Andalusians. In a very little time it became clear that the Spanish Muslims were by no means sufficiently harmonious or sufficiently resolute to be capable of defending themselves. The Christians were in possession of the castle of Aledo near Murcia from which they conducted constant raids against them. In 1088 al-Muatamid personally visited Yusuf in Morocco in order to persuade him to cross the Straits again. In 1089 the Almoravid, acceding to the request, crossed for a second time and advanced on Aledo with the support of al-Muatamid and the rulers of Granada, Almeria and Murcia. When a quarrel arose be-tween al-Muatamid and the Murcian prince, and was decided in Muatamid's favour by Yusuf as arbitrator, the Murcian ceased to co-operate. Shortly after this the arrival of a Christian relief force com-pelled Yusuf to withdraw, bitterly disillusioned with the conduct of the Andalusian princes. By now he was receiving pressing appeals from the religious leaders of the Spanish Muslims who complained not only of the Christian attacks but also of the dissolute lives, extravagance, and un-Islamic conduct of their own princes. There is nothing to suggest that Yusuf had all the time been inspired by ambition to extend his own rule in Spain. In the new circum-stances however the pleadings of the men of religion, combined with his own experience at Aledo, must have convinced him that the only hope of preserving Muslim Spain from the Christians was to assert his own authority over the whole area. He first secured a ruling from the religious authorities of his own country (later confirmed by eminent men of religion in the orient) to the effect that the Andalusian princes were dissolute, that they neglected their religious duties, imposed illegal taxes, and allied themselves with the infidels. This being so, they were unworthy to reign, the *fatwa* said, and Yusuf was released from any commitments which he had undertaken towards them. Fortified with this pronouncement Yusuf crossed the Straits for the third time, in 1090, and proceeded to depose the King of Granada who had resumed payment of tribute to Alfonso and his brother, the ruler of Almeria. The King of Granada yielded with a good grace and was rewarded with a suitable position in Morocco. Being a man of literary tastes he took the opportunity to compose his memoirs which give a vivid and first-hand account of these events as they were witnessed by one of the principal participants.

Alarmed at the fate of the two princes, al-Muatamid refused to meet Yusuf to discuss the latter's demand that he should abolish taxation inconsistent with Muslim law and join in the Holy War against the Christians. When Yusuf attacked his domains, he turned again to Alfonso for aid while telling Yusuf that it was he who had forced him to do so. Alfonso was, however, in no position to help, and after a heroic defence by al-Muatamid and the citizens, his capital Seville fell to Yusuf's troops. The unfortunate prince spent his few remaining years as prisoner at Aghmat where he bewailed his fate in verse as melodious as that in which he had formerly celebrated his splendour and the delights of Seville.

By degrees the Almoravids took over the rest of Muslim Spain;

in 1102 after the death of the Cid, Valencia was regained from the Christians. From this time for about a century and a half the rulers of Morocco were rulers of Spain also, though Almoravid rule itself lasted only till 1143. Yusuf died in 1107 at the age of more than ninety and was succeeded by his son Ali, a young man of twenty-three whose mother was a Christian slave. His succession was secured without serious difficulty and his reign lasted for thirty-seven years. He was by no means an unworthy prince, though with him piety became a cloistered virtue rather than the open-air manliness of his father. The earlier years of his reign were marked by considerable successes. Aledo was recovered from the Christians and there were victories in Portugal. On the other hand Saragossa was lost to the King of Aragon in 1118 and repeated attempts to recover Toledo were unsuccessful.

Ali, like his father, took the title of *Amir al-Muslimin*, considering his followers as Almoravids, and he followed his father's path in waging the Holy War, defending his country and inspiring respect in its enemies. His intentions were excellent and his conduct irreproachable. In his nobility of character and hatred of injustice he was more like a hermit and ascetic than an absolute monarch. Having a strong predilection for men of law (*fiqh*) and of religion, he decided nothing without hearing their advice.[4]

Ali's saintly character was as ill adapted to the circumstances of his time as was that of our own King Henry VI to his. It appears that the other princes of the royal family despised Ali for his deference to his religious advisers and began to act independently of him. At the same time a serious menace to the régime was developing as the result of the appearance of a new religious reformer among the Masmouda Berbers of the Atlas. The historian quoted above thus describes the latter portion of Ali's reign.

The authority of *Amir al-Muslimin* was much impaired and conditions in the state greatly deteriorated when control began to pass into the hands of the Almoravid notables and they made public pretensions to independent authority, claiming in a body that they were better than the Amir and had more right to rule. Their women, who were consulted in every matter of importance, were largely responsible for this. The women of the Lamtuna and the Masufa (two leading tribes) took to associating with people of bad character such as wine-merchants and cabaratiers while the Amir took increasingly little interest in public affairs, concerning himself only with devotion and the ascetic life. He would fast by day and keep vigil at night, and while this reflected credit on his personal character it resulted in his totally neglecting his subjects' affairs. In consequence there were widespread disturbances in al-Andalus which began to lapse into the condition (of subjection to Christian aggression) which it had been in formerly, particularly after Ibn Tumart initiated his agitation in the Sous.[4]

These lines were written in the days of the succeeding dynasty and have clearly been affected by the propaganda which they carried on in order to discredit their predecessors. Nevertheless, the fact that the movement initated by Ibn Tumart was able to put an end to Almoravid rule within two years of Ali's death certainly indicates a very serious failing on the part of that monarch, at least in the latter part of his reign.

There has been much discussion among modern historians concerning the merits or defects of Almoravid rule in Spain. It has been suggested that their subservience to fanatical and ignorant religious leaders destroyed liberty of thought and that their intolerance made impossible the continued existence there of the arabized Spanish Christians known as Mozarabs.

On the first point, there is no doubt that the Almoravids appeared to the Muslims of Spain as uncultured, rough, and primitive. There are numbers of pieces of satirical verse and anecdotes which illustrate this. It is also true that at the instigation of religious fanatics the works of the great Iraqi religious reformer, al-Ghazali, were publicly burned in Seville during the period of Almoravid rule. Against this however we must remember that the censorship and the burning of books in Spain preceded the rule of the Almoravids and continued for centuries after it, both under Muslim and under Christian rule. The luxurious and luxury-loving al-Muatadid, al-Muatamid's predecessor as ruler of Seville, had the works of Ibn Hazm, almost as distinguished a writer on religion as al-Ghazali himself, publicly burnt, on the pretext of heresy. On the second point it is not fair to hold the Almoravids responsible for the misfortune of the arabized Christians of Andalusia. Their lot as subjects of a Muslim state

58

began to become impossible as soon as Christians from the north began to raid the south and to persuade them to act as a fifth column. From that moment it was inevitable that they should be regarded with suspicion and it was almost inevitable that the decision would be taken to deport large numbers of them to the south of the Straits. A measure of tolerance is indicated by the fact that the Almoravids made use of a force of Christian troops who were stationed normally in Marrakesh. Their commander was a Catalan named Reverter and they appear to have been free to practice their religion. It is not certain what percentage were prisoners who accepted such service, what percentage were arabized Christians from Spain, and what percentage volunteers recruited in the Christian Spanish states with the permission of their rulers, as was certainly the case at a later date. From the story of the Cid we know that it was customary in Almoravid times for Christian notables, who were for some reason dissatisfied in their own country, to take service with a Muslim prince; no doubt less exalted personages did so also.

It is not at all clear that serious literature suffered under Almoravid rule, though of course the abolition of all the little states, most of whose rulers had delighted to surround themselves with poets and panegyrists, must have greatly reduced patronage of a certain type of literary production. How great a value is to be given to its loss is another question. The Almoravids are in any case not to be blamed for the schizophrenic condition of the Muslims of Spain, divided as they were into self-indulgent notables and a narrow-minded and often fanatical clergy.

Nor is there evidence that Almoravid rule brought a lessening of the standards of administration; on the contrary it must have put an end to a good many abuses due to the licentious life and extravagant pleasures of the princes.

The gold coinage of the Almoravids indeed had such prestige that King Alfonso VIII of Castile made Christian imitations of them, with Arabic lettering, for use in his own domains. The inscriptions on the Muslim coins gave the date in the Muslim era; Alfonso's *maravedis* (a Spanish equivalent of *murabitis*) gave a Spanish Christian date. The Muslim coins bore the text:

Ali ibn Yusuf, Commander of the Muslims. There is no God but God and Muhammad is the Prophet of God. The Commander of the Faithful is the Imam Abdullah the Abbasid. Whoever chooses another worship than Islam it shall not be received of him and he will be among the wretched in the other world.

The Castilian coins bore a precisely parallel text, Christian Gospel phrases replacing the Muslim and Quranic.

Alfonso, son of Sancho, Commander of the Catholics. In the name of the Father, the Son, and the Holy Spirit, the one God. The Imam of the Church of the Messiah is the Pope at Rome. He who has faith and has been baptised will be saved.

Light on administration under the Almoravids in Spain is to be found in a contemporary treatise on municipal government in Seville under the Almoravids. From this it is apparent that there was a Moroccan Almoravid governor who no doubt had Moroccans on his staff, but in general municipal administration seems to have been carried on as before by local officials. In Seville, and also in Valencia, there is evidence to show that the Almoravid garrisons, who were easily distinguished by their veils, were kept very much apart from the public, rather as troops in foreign bases are today.

When we turn to Morocco, what is striking is the very rapid assimilation by the Almoravids of Andalusian civilization and the use made by them of Spanish Muslim architects and engineers. From this epoch, for the first time since the Roman period, we find architectural monuments of importance. Much of the Qarawiyin mosque in Fez dates from the Almoravids; another interesting monument of the period, known as the Qubbat al-Barudiya, has recently been uncovered in Marrakesh. The finest surviving Almoravid monument is however the great mosque in Tlemsen, now outside Moroccan territory. Unlike the Moroccan mosques this is open to the non-Muslim visitor and gives a vivid impression of what the Almoravids could achieve in this type of construction.

Finally it is to the credit of the Almoravids as Muslim rulers that without their intervention Muslim Spain would almost certainly have succumbed to the Christians 200 years sooner than it did.

16 This bronze bust is of Juba II, the king of Mauritania in the first century A.D. In A.D. 41 Mauritania was converted into a Roman province.

17 and 18 Juba II governed from Volubilis where this mosaic (*above*) and bronze dog (*below*) were found.

19 The ruins of the palace at Volubilis which was later taken over by the Roman governor.

20 and 21 The Almoravid empire of the tenth century included Muslim Spain known as al-Andalus. These coins (*left*) are Spanish Christian imitations of the Muslim Almoravid originals (*left below*) as a result of this conquest.

22 and 23 The Andalusian civilization in turn influenced the architecture of the period. This is the Qarawiyin mosque at Fez (*left and above*).

24 Originally Fez consisted of two separate cities called the Qarawiyin and the Andalusian quarters which were joined together by the Almoravid ruler Yusuf ibn Tashfin. This is the gateway of the Andalus mosque in the Andalusian quarter.

25 Springs were utilized for irrigation and by the end of the eleventh century many householders had their own mills and running water. This water wheel is at Bu Jeloud, where the Almoravid governor once lived.

26 During the course of Morocco's history each new dynasty left its influence on
Fez – the centre of religious, commercial and intellectual life.

27 The sanctuary of Maulay Idris I, the founder of the Moroccan state in the ninth century, outside Fez, has long been a place of pilgrimage for Muslims.

28 and 29 This ancient mosque (*above right*) is one of many at Maulay Idris and is a striking contrast to the modern mosque near by (*right*).

4 The Almohad Caliphate and the Beni Merin

THE BERBER-SPEAKING PEOPLE, known as the Masmouda, who inhabited the High Atlas and the Anti-Atlas farther south never had any love for the nomadic Sanhaja. As we have seen, it was partly as a protection against them that Yusuf chose the site of Marrakesh rather than Aghmat for his capital. In spite of this precaution it was the Masmouda who eventually overthrew the Almoravid régime replacing it with their own. This achievement was the work of a Berber-speaking theologian, born either in the Atlas or the Anti-Atlas, named Muhammad ibn Tumart. Unlike Abdullah Yasin, Ibn Tumart was not merely a religious reformer of puritan outlook, but a subtle and learned theologian who claimed to be the promised Mahdi; his followers called themselves al-Muwahhadun or unitarians, people who emphasize the oneness of God. It is due to their influence that public and private correspondence in Morocco has since their time been commonly introduced by the formula 'Praise be to God, the unique'.

It seems to have been in 1107, the year of Yusuf ibn Tashfin's death, that Ibn Tumart set off for the east in search of knowledge in the great Muslim theological schools of the day. Ten years later he returned to Morocco. On his journey back along North Africa to Marrakesh he was accompanied by a disciple who years later wrote an account of the journey. By a happy chance the manuscript of most of this, like that of the memoirs of King Abdullah of Granada, was recently recovered by Professor Lévi-Provençal and gives us a vivid and authentic picture of the early period of the Almohad movement.[5]

In the mutilated manuscript the account begins with Ibn Tumart in Tunis. He was accompanied by three followers of whom one, Abu Bakr ibn Ali al-Sanhaji, known by the nickname of al-Baidaq or the Pawn, is the author of the account. From his narrative, it is evident that al-Baidaq had something of the same naïve devotion to his master which some of the Galilean disciples had to Jesus of Nazareth; he sometimes presents in a miraculous light an episode which is capable of a natural interpretation. Al-Baidaq seems to have acted as groom for his master. When a widow woman with whom they lodged at Bougie gave the master a grey filly with a white belly as packhorse to carry their scanty equipment, al-Baidaq was put in charge of her. Years later, when the Mahdi was wounded in a battle with the Almoravid forces south of Marrakesh, it was al-Baidaq who helped him on to his riding mule, Tamweemaq, held the bridle, and led his master back to safety, while another follower carried his lance and shield.

From Tunis their journey took them first to Constantine and then to Bougie. In each city where they stayed Ibn Tumart acted in the traditional role of an Islamic religious reformer, 'reproving what is disapproved and enjoining what is good' according to a phrase in the Quran. He would take up his residence either at the Mosque or at the house of some pious believer, spend much time in discussion with the men of learning of the locality, and periodically engage in public reproof of offenders. In Bougie he forbade the male inhabitants to put gilded laces in their shoes, to wear turbans customary in the pre-Islamic period, or to appear in a type of garment resembling a woman's dress. During the fête marking the end of Ramadan he was scandalized to see men and women walking together. Forcing his way between them he gave blows right and left with his stick. After this he was advised by a friendly son of the ruler to take up his residence outside the town; here a little oratory was built for him. One day however when walking near the quay he spilt on the ground the wine which was being sold there, proclaiming that dates were the food of Muslims, wine that of infidels. When the police struck him, asking by what authority he did this, he replied, 'By God's and his Prophet's.' It was at the village outside Bougie that

Ibn Tumart was joined by his most famous disciple. One night, al-Baidaq tells us, he listened to Ibn Tumart speaking after completing his prayers. 'On all occasions' he was saying, 'praise should be given to God, whose might and wisdom are the sole source of victory. Tomorrow there will come to you a man in search of knowledge; blessed be he who acknowledges him, woe to him who disowns him.' On the following morning, as they were seated in the mosque, a young man was seen approaching. As he was opposite him Ibn Tumart lifted his head. 'Come in, my son,' he said. The young man entered and prepared to take his place among the crowd, but on Ibn Tumart's insistence came close to him. 'Your name, young man?' the Mahdi asked. 'Abdelmumin.' 'Your father is called Ali?' 'Yes.' Those present glanced at one another in surprise. 'Where do you come from?' 'From the neighbourhood of Tlemsen, from the Kumya country, near the coast.' 'From Tajra, I think?' said the Mahdi. 'Yes.' The astonishment of those present increased. 'Where are you making for, my son?', the Mahdi went on. 'To the East, master, in search of knowledge.' 'The knowledge which you are proposing to seek in the east, you have found here in the west.' From this moment Abd al-Mumin became the inseparable companion of the Mahdi and in due time his successor and the ruler of a great empire. From the writings of the great Arab historian Ibn Khaldun, it appears that the students in Tlemsen had in fact sent Abd al-Mumin to Bougie to invite Ibn Tumart to come to Tlemsen as their teacher. In this case it would not be surprising that the Mahdi should have had foreknowledge of his coming.

However this may be, it was not long before stories with a miraculous colouring began to be told of Abd al-Mumin himself. It was said that when his mother was pregnant with him, she dreamed that fire came forth from her womb and spread to the four quarters of heaven. Shortly before his birth she fell asleep in the fields while her husband was harvesting, and two swarms of bees settled upon her body without harming her. Soon after his birth she was again in the fields to glean. Having put the baby down, bees came again, more numerous than the first time, and settled on the child, only later to rise again and fly off in two groups, one to the east and one to the west, a prophecy, as it was believed, of his later far-flung Caliphate.

It is difficult to be sure when in fact Ibn Tumart and Abd al-Mumin first conceived the idea that their religious reform would be accompanied by the substitution of Almoravid rule by their own, but it may well have been on this journey. Many sayings quoted by al-Baidaq suggest this. Certainly the idea must have been already dormant in Abd al-Mumin's unconscious mind, if it be true, as al-Baidaq reports, that he one night dreamed that he was eating out of the same dish as the Almoravid ruler, Ali ibn Tashfin, that he felt a ravening hunger, wrested the dish from him, and himself ate up all that was on it.

Having left Bougie the journey took them through the plain behind Algiers, past Miliana, through the Warsenis to Relizane and on to Tlemsen. On entering Tlemsen the Mahdi encountered a marriage party taking a bride to her husband's house. She was riding on a saddle, preceded by a 'procession with reprehensible diversions'. The Mahdi broke the drums and the musical instruments, put an end to the 'immoral scene', and forced the bride to descend from her mount.

On other occasions he used his reputation for sanctity to intervene successfully against oppressive rulers, as when certain villagers in the Rif complained to him of the excessive fine inflicted on them by a Wazir, one of whose ostriches they had killed. At another village, on the contrary, where men and women were jointly celebrating some festivity with music, his interference produced the retort that such was their custom. 'You look after your own morals,' they said, 'and we will look after ours.' Having arrived at Fez, Ibn Tumart, whom the local men of the law referred to as the '*faqih* from the Sous' received a favourable welcome. One day he told seven disciples to cut sticks from the non-fruit-bearing figs by the river and to hide them under their cloaks. Thus equipped he took them to the quarters where musical instruments were sold and set them to break the drums, castanets, flutes, violins, guitars, and lutes. On complaining to the judge, the merchants were told that Ibn Tumart had justifica-tion in the Law for his prohibition and that they were at fault in selling such things. After passing through Meknès and Salé (where al-Baidaq for the first time realized that Ibn Tumart could speak Berber as well as Arabic) they finally reached Marrakesh, probably in the year 1121. By now Ibn Tumart was a much discussed personality, with warm supporters and equally vehement critics. The obviously sincere piety of Ali ibn Tashfin was clearly an embarrassment to his propaganda; to counteract this Ibn Tumart relied on the assertion of his theological learning and of his own authority. He betook himself to the principal mosque on the Friday when he knew that the Amir would be there. Approaching the spot where the Amir was seated, with his ministers before him, he was (according to al-Baidaq) instructed by them to greet the Amir with the respect due to a Commander of the Faithful. 'Where is the Amir?' he replied, 'I see nothing but veiled girls.' The gentle Ali removed his veil, remarking that Ibn Tumart was quite right. 'The Caliphate is God's, not yours, Ali ibn Yusuf,' Ibn Tumart told him. 'If you are a true Imam you should get up from that dyed garment, I mean that black mantle on which you are sitting.' As the Amir drew it from under him and handed it back to its owner, he asked Ibn Tumart what objection there was to its being dyed. 'Impure substances are used to dye it,' said Ibn Tumart who then made his way out of the mosque, not returning till the congregation had dispersed.

The deeply pious Ali was unwilling to take action in spite of Ibn Tumart's increasing insolence. Matters came to a head however when the latter met Ali's sister, Sura, riding unveiled, as was the custom of the Almoravid ladies, and not only rebuked her for this but struck her horse so that she was thrown to the ground. The matter was discussed in Ali's council some of whom urged Ibn Tumart's immediate arrest and execution as a potentially dangerous rebel. Ali however would consent only to his banishment from the city. Ibn Tumart thereupon left Marrakesh and took up his residence in the High Atlas at Tinmel, today a green clearing beside the mountain road from Marrakesh to Tarudant but then a highly inaccessible mountain refuge. Here he organized the local Berbers into a closely knit religious and military community, capable of gradually extending its authority over the neighbouring areas. In doing so Ibn Tumart was not slow to shed blood, as in the case of the famous

73

Forty Day Purge when hundreds of the hesitant were labelled as 'hypocrites' and executed. At the head of the community were the Ten; next to them the Council of Fifty. Ibn Tumart himself led an extremely austere life. He fed simply, wore plain and old clothes, and took no interest in women. Religious duties were enforced with a severity equal to that of the early Almoravids; the believers were taught to listen to lengthy sermons; absolute obedience was exacted from the rank and file, to the extent of killing their own relations if so ordered. To teach Arabic prayers to Berbers he would give each member of a Berber group a word of the prayer as his name. Standing in a row in the appropriate order each man would then repeat his name so that the whole formed the words of the prayer, which they thus acquired by memory. The essentials of his doctrine were circulated in brochures which were written in Berber as well as in Arabic. In his teaching he emphasized the speedy coming of the promised Mahdi, quoting the relevant prophecies, until one day his followers by a sudden illumination exclaimed, 'You . . . you are the Mahdi, the one exempt from sin.' On the other hand he took pains to show them that he was a man like themselves, with all the needs of other men for food and other bodily necessities.

Once the Atlas area was under control, the Almohads began to attack the Almoravids whom they nicknamed the anthropo-morphists (al-mujassimun) on the grounds that since they did not permit interpretations of such expressions in the Quran as 'the face of God' they must imply that God had a body like a man. About the year 1130 they ventured to attack the Almoravids in the plain, inflicted several defeats on them and attacked Marrakesh. The Mahdi, who was ill, did not accompany them and in a battle at al-Buhaira, the Almoravid forces which included Reverter and his Christian troops totally defeated them, killing the Almohad commander. Al-Baidaq was detailed to bring the news to the Mahdi. 'What about Abd al-Mumin?' asked the latter. 'He is safe.' 'Praise be to the Lord of the Universe. The situation can be restored then. Is he wounded?' 'In the right thigh.' 'There is no power save in God,' replied the Mahdi. 'Nothing irrevocable has happened. Get back and tell them so. There is no cause to fear.' Two months later the

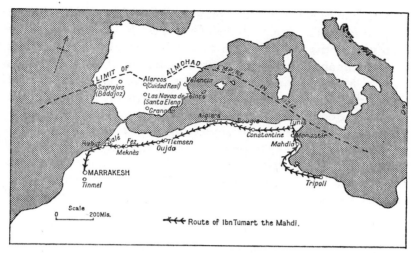

The Almohad Empire in 1212

Mahdi died. His death seems to have been long kept secret possibly for as much as two years, while the succession of Abd al-Mumin, himself not an Atlas Berber but a Rifi, was being secured.

It has seemed worth while to relate the early history of the Almohad movement at length because the Almohads were the greatest of all Moroccan rulers – great rulers by any standards. The story is very characteristic of Islamic and Moroccan life, as it was and to some extent still is, and it has lost little of its relevance today.

Fifteen years more fighting followed the Mahdi's death before the Almoravid régime finally collapsed. In 1144 Reverter was killed while commanding a mixed Christian-Muslim force in the north; only three of the Christians survived on this occasion and we know their names – Juan, Gaston, and Adrian – which indicate clearly that they were from Christian Spain. Ali's son, and short-lived successor, Tashfin ibn Ali was killed in the next year, his horse falling over a precipice while he was trying to escape from Ceuta on a dark night. Fez was taken after an eight months siege and Marrakesh two years later, in 1147. A wholesale slaughter of Almoravids and their supporters in the city followed. The nominal ruler, a boy called Ishaq, was brought before Abd al-Mumin and pleaded for mercy, being rebuked for this by the Almoravid *Wazir* who was captive with him. Abd al-Mumin proposed to spare him but an Almohad Sheikh cried out, 'Ho, ho, the Almohads! Here's Abd al-Mumin setting himself against us. He's going to raise the lion's whelp to oppose us.' Abd al-Mumin remained silent and the unfortunate boy was led off to execution.

Abd al-Mumin and his great successors, Abu Yaacub (1162–89) and al-Mansur (1189–98), established their rule over all the previous Almoravid realms and extended the frontiers in North Africa to Tunis and to Tripoli. In Tunisia the Almohad viceroys were eventually to found a dynasty which ruled there till the coming of the Turks in 1574.

In all, Almohad rule lasted 125 years (1143–1268), of which the last fifty were a time of rapidly increasing disaster. We cannot follow these events in detail here. We can only note that like the Almoravids the early puritanism of the Almohads was very soon modified by the influence of Muslim Spain. On first capturing Fez, Abd al-Mumin had marked his disapproval of the Almoravids in two ways. One was by destroying the fortress which they had built at Bu Jeloud. 'We don't need fortresses,' said Abd al-Mumin, 'our fortresses are our swords and our justice.' The other was to cover with plaster the decoration of the Almoravid mosque, the Qarawiyin, which they found too florid. Soon however Abd al-Mumin was himself to build an equally handsome mosque at Tinmel, to commemorate the part which the site had played in the early history of the Almohads and to serve as mausoleum for the Mahdi. This building still exists, though it suffered from unhappy restoration in the early days of the protectorate. For the traveller in Spain or Morocco today, the greatest evidence of the artistic achievements of the Almohads are the great minarets, the Kutubia at Marrakesh and the sister towers, the Giralda at Seville and the unfinished tower of the Hassan Mosque at Rabat, built within ten years of one another, by one or more Spanish Muslim architects. Equally impressive are some of their fortifications and their gatetways, notably Bab Aguenau at Marrakesh, and Bab al-Ruah and the gateway of the Oudaia citadel at Rabat, founded as a subsidiary capital between the Moroccan capital in Marrakesh and the Spanish capital in Seville. Oddly enough one of the finest extant examples of Almohad art is the decoration of the Chapel of Las Claustrillas at Burgos in northern Spain. Built by a Christian king about 1200, it is certain that he either employed Muslim workmen or arabized Christians (Mozarabs) from Andalusia. In the same way, another splendid example of Almohad decoration is to be seen in the former synagogue at Toledo, known today as Santa Maria la Blanca.

The great contrast in intellectual eminence between Abdullah Yasin and Muhammad ibn Tumart was reflected in the intellectual quality of the Almohad leadership. While the mass of Almohad supporters were Berber-speakers, there was a greater proportion of educated persons, that is people with a good Arabic culture, in the higher levels than there had been among the Almoravids. In 1160 Abd al-Mumin held a great assembly in Gibraltar to which he summoned 'the notables of the country, his captains and great personages, princes from al-Andalus and from the African shore of the Straits, in a fashion that no king before him had done. For the first time he summoned also the poets without their having to secure previous permission'.[6] This was the beginning of an epoch in which the learning of Muslim Spain, at that time equal or superior to western learning elsewhere, was diffused in Morocco also.

Almohad dislike of the presence of Jews in their realms had indeed the effect of promoting the disappearance of Jewish men of learning and physicians. This was the case of the Maimonides family in Cordoba who like other Jews were faced with the alternatives of professing the Muslim faith or of exile. They first opted to move into Muslim Spanish towns which had not yet submitted to the Almohads. Later they apparently decided for the first option, the legitimacy of which was defended by Maimonides, and moved to Fez where there appears to have been a considerable Jewish community secretly practising Judaism while outwardly professing Islam. Apart from the questionable morality of this proceeding, the dangers of discovery were great and the family finally decided to move to Cairo where they could remain in an area of the Arab culture to which they were accustomed, and at the same time openly practise their Jewish faith.

Of the famous Muslims of comparable qualifications, however, Ibn Tufail (1110–85) attended on the Caliph Abu Yaacub and introduced to him the equally famous Ibn Rushd (Averrhoes). When Ibn Rushd was first presented the Caliph asked him whether the universe was eternal or created. When Ibn Rushd in some embarrassment excused himself, fearing the difficulty of explaining such a complicated issue to the monarch, Abu Yaacub expounded the problem himself, quoting Aristotle and Muslim authorities with such mastery that Ibn Rushd no longer hesitated to give his own view. For this he was rewarded with a robe of honour, a riding horse, and a monetary gratification. He later succeeded Ibn Tufail as court physician. His philosophical works were however at one moment burnt, on the grounds of a reference in his discussion of Greek philosophy to the 'goddess' Venus, which was held to be heretical; though some people said that the real cause was a reference to the Almohad sovereigns, held to be insulting, as 'kings of the Berbers'. His medical, mathematical, and astronomical works were in any case exempted from the order and he himself was restored to favour some years later. In fact scientific and medical knowledge reached its highest point in Andalusia during this period. When translated under the aegis of the King of Castile into Latin and Castilian a century later, some of the works composed under the Almohad rule became textbooks which were used in European universities for several centuries.

One action of the first Almohad Caliph, Abd al-Mumin, is generally considered to have had unfortunate results for Morocco. In the eleventh century a Fatimid Caliph in Cairo launched on North Africa two predatory Arab tribes, the Beni Hilal and the Beni Sulaim; there they became an element of disorder and destruc-tion. When Abd al-Mumin defeated them in Tunisia in 1152 he deported many of them to Morocco where he used them as troops against rebellious local tribes. The unfortunate result was the intro-duction of nomad destructiveness into a hitherto settled agricultural area. Another result was the conversion of a Berber-speaking into an Arabic-speaking area. Another Arab tribe, the Maaqil, who reached Mauritania converted the whole former Almoravid desert territory into an area of Arab speech and indeed into a centre of Arab and Islamic learning among the nomads.

Signs of Almohad decadence appeared suddenly at the end of the reign of the fourth Caliph, Muhammad al-Nasir (1198–1213). After thirteen years successful reign, this Caliph resolved to make a supreme effort against the King of Castile and his allies. According to reports which reached the papal chancellery he proposed to advance into other Christian lands. This news caused great alarm among the neighbouring Christian princes, and an English chronicler, Walter of Coventry, reports that it seemed as if he intended to 'overwhelm all Christendom'. Innocent III, then Pope, sent letters to the Spanish Christian princes urging them to unite against this threat. It happened that this was at a moment when King John of England, having successfully reduced the Irish and Welsh to obedience, was preparing an expedition to recover Normandy from the French King. Angevin-English troops were to attack France from Aquitaine in the south-west while their allies attacked from the north-east. The threat of a Muslim advance made it essential for King John to protect his rear. Three ambassadors were therefore despatched 'in great haste' to Muhammad al-Nasir, who was in Seville in the early summer of 1211. In the account given by Matthew Paris the Caliph, who is described as 'Miramolin' (*Amir al-Muminin*) 'the great king of Morocco, Africa [i.e. eastern Algeria and Tunisia] and Spain' is said to have rejected King John's proposal with contumely. It is, however, possible that this is a misrepresentation and that agreement was reached for some sort of co-operation if Muhammad al-Nasir should succeed in crossing the Pyrenees. Any such possibility was however completely destroyed when the Caliph suffered a crushing defeat at Las Navas de Tolosa (al-Uqab) on the border of Andalusia and Castile in July 1212. The defeated Caliph retired to Marrakesh where he died in the following year. From this moment Almohad power decayed rapidly, Valencia being lost to King Jaime of Aragon in 1228; and Cordoba and Seville to King Ferdinand of Castile in 1236 and 1248 respectively.

A number of interesting features mark the period of over fifty years between the death of Muhammad al-Nasir and the final Almohad collapse in 1268. One was in the field of religion. Orthodox in most respects, the Almohad régime was heretical in supporting the claim of Ibn Tumart to be the Mahdi – a claim which was never accepted outside the Almohad domains and ignored by very many people within them. Already from the time of the second Caliph, Abu Yaacub, the claim was somewhat played down, though a deter-mined effort was made to impose the Mahdi's teaching in its other aspects. The process continued and one of the later Caliph's, al-Mamun (1226-31), actually mounted the pulpit in the great mosque at Marrakesh and informed the assembled congregation that Ibn Tumart was not the Mahdi but an impostor and that the only true Mahdi was the Messiah, Isa (Jesus) son of Mary. This it is true occurred when the Almohad régime was in a state of extreme decadence and the Calpih had had to borrow 12,000 Christian troops from the Castilian King at the cost of a ruinous surrender of territory. The final result of Almohad rule in the field of religion was to carry on the task of creating an orthodox Muslim community out of the various peoples of Morocco.

Like the Almoravids, the Almohads made extensive use of Christian troops, taking over the remnants of Reverter's forces after the final Almoravid collapse. They also employed eminent Christian Spaniards and Portuguese as military advisers. In the reign of the second Caliph, the Portuguese adventurer, Giraldo Giraldes, whose exploits in capturing Evora and other cities from the Muslims, have caused him to be called the Portuguese Cid, took service with the Almohads when they made peace with Portugal in 1173. He was actually made Governor of the Sus where, however, he betrayed the trust placed in him and so brought about his own death. In the reign of the third Caliph, a Castilian noble, Dom Pedro Fernandez de Castro, was in charge of 'army administration and captain general' in Marrakesh, to use the probably rather misleading language of a Portuguese chronicler. Another ally, or satellite, of the Almohads, King Sancho of Navarre (who was also ally of King John and brother-in-law of John's predecessor, Richard Cœur-de-Lion), undoubtedly spent at least two years in Muslim territory from 1199 and according to one account took part in Almohad expeditions. In the time of al-Mustansir, who succeeded Muhammad al-Nasir in 1213, another Dom Pedro, brother of the reigning King of Portugal with whom he had quarrelled, served as military adviser in Marra-kesh. He and quite a community of Christians were there when five Franciscan missionaries arrived who had been despatched by St Francis himself. These made a point of publicly insulting the Muslim faith and the Prophet Muhammad. The Caliph twice despatched them under escort to Ceuta so that they could return to Christendom, but on each occasion they escaped and returned to Marrakesh. Finally the young Caliph, who was eighteen years old at the time (and fond of bull-fighting which was the cause of his death three years later), found this provocation intolerable. After first offering the Franciscans wives and employment if they would accept Islam, he executed them (1219). Dom Pedro nevertheless was allowed to collect their remains and transport them to Coimbra where they were credited with working miracles. In spite of the provocation which led to this martyrdom, and to that of seven other Franciscans in Ceuta in the following year, later Almohad sovereigns had within twelve years sanctioned the establishment of a Bishopric, nominally in Fez but actually in Marrakesh. The first Bishop, the Franciscan Agnello, was appointed by Gregory V and reached Marrakesh in 1233. The Church and Convent of St Mary were situated near the Almohad palace, no doubt for security, as was also the case with the Jewry. Nominally the Bishopric continued till 1639; but from about 1400 the Bishops lived in Seville in a quarter known as the Barrio de Marruecos and appear rarely to have gone farther than Ceuta which was in Christian hands from 1415.

As in the preceding cases the replacement of the Almohads by their successors involved several decades of dissension and civil war. The new rulers, known as the Beni Merin, were another group of Berber tribes; this time however they came from the east of the country beyond Taza, at the northern end of the great semicircular plateaux which we have described as the outer Morocco. Though the founder of the dynasty, Abd al-Haqq, was a charismatic leader of outstanding piety, credited with possessing *baraka* in a high degree, the Beni Merin did not come into power on the crest of a religious reform. They are therefore simply known by their tribal name. In the religious field they forwarded the movement for the return to orthodoxy. By campaigning in Spain the earlier Merinids achieved the religious aura which attached to those who took part in the Holy War; and they distinguished themselves also by their multiplication of pious foundations, above all of numerous *madrasas*, or hostels for students, which they established in Fez and elsewhere. In the later period of their rule they restored the sanctuary of Maulay Idris in Fez (1437) and gave the sanction of their authority to the 'invention' (in the hagiographic sense) of an uncorrupted body and its identification as that of Maulay Idris II. This led to a phenomenal development of the shrine as a place of pilgrimage.

The most eminent of the dynasty were Abu Yahya (1244–58), Abu Yusuf Yaacub (1258–86), Abu Yaacub Yusuf (1286–1307), and Abu al-Hassan (1330–51). Merinid rule nominally continued till 1465, though for thirty-five years already power had passed into the hands of the Beni Wattas, who first made the office of *Wazir* hereditary in their family and then became officially rulers from 1465 to 1554.

It was during the reign of these sovereigns that there was born in Tangier a boy known as Abu Abdullah Muhammad ibn Batuta who was to become the greatest of all Muslim travellers. Between 1325 and 1355 he travelled through Arabia and the Middle East, reaching as far as Diarbekr. He then sailed down the Red Sea to Aden and thence down the East African coast to Mombasa and Kilwa. Later he crossed the Black Sea and went on to Uzbekistan, India, and China. In 1349 he was back in Morocco, after an absence of twenty-four years. Happy to see his native land again he remarked that 'though the Moroccan *dirhams* are small, you can buy a lot with them', a comment that would not probably be made today about the *dirham* coinage recently introduced. Not content with what he had already seen, he now went first north to visit the Kingdom of Granada and then south to Timbuctu, returning by Hoggar and Tuat. He died in his native town, Tangier, years later at the age of seventy-three.

On Ibn Batuta's return to Fez from Timbuctu in 1354, the Merinid ruler Abu Inan provided him with a secretary to take down the account of his travels. During this stay he can hardly have failed to meet the famous historian of North Africa, Ibn Khaldun, since the latter was then in Abu Inan's service and frequented his literary gatherings. Ibn Khaldun was not himself Moroccan, but was born and brought up in Tunis, being a member of a Spanish Muslim family from Seville which had taken refuge there.

The early Beni Merin endeavoured to restore Moroccan sovereignty over the eastern Maghrib and in 1348 Abu al-Hassan actually occupied Tunis. This success was however ephemeral. Even less success attended Merinid efforts to restore the shattered Muslim position in Spain. In 1264 the capture of Jerez in the west by the King of Castile, followed in 1269 by the capture in the east of Cartagena by the King of Aragon, left the little Kingdom of Granada the only area in Spain which was not under Christian rule. This independence it was only able to preserve by playing off the Christian kings against one another and against other Muslim monarchs. This diplomatic game was very intricate. In 1274 the Moroccan ruler Abu Yusuf went in person to Barcelona to negotiate an alliance with the Aragonese King. In return for trade concessions he secured the service of 500 Christian knights and a number of ships. This enabled him to suppress a revolt in Ceuta and so utilize that port as a base for an attack on Castile, when in the following year his aid was sought by the King of Granada. Like Yusuf ibn Tashfin, the Moroccan ruler would not move until he had Tangier also under his control. He then crossed the Straits, advanced to the neighbourhood of Cordoba, and defeated a strong Christian relief force, after which he returned to Morocco. Two years later after a similar expedition he displeased his Granadan ally by securing for himself the suzerainty over Malaga, hitherto dependent on Granada. In consequence the Granadan King made advances to Castile, regained Malaga by suborning the Merinid governor, and encouraged a revolt against the Merinid ruler in Morocco. In view of these Muslim dissensions, the Castilian monarch proceeded to besiege Algeciras; an action which so alarmed the Granadan that he

83

immediately reversed his alliances and lent his fleet to the Moroccan ruler for an attack on the Christians. In the resulting naval battle of Algeciras the combined Muslim fleets defeated the Christian fleet and relieved the city. It was this or a later siege of Algeciras in which the knight in the prologue of Chaucer's *Canterbury Tales* took part, before crossing the Straits 'to ride in Belmarie' by which term the domains of the Beni Merin were described by the English of that age. In 1282 however there was a fresh transformation scene when the Castilian King Alfonso X was faced with a rebellion by his son and heir and found it necessary to seek Moroccan assistance. This he secured by handing over the crown of Castile as security for a loan of 100,000 dinars. The Merinid ruler then crossed the Straits and advanced far inland.

A curious letter is still extant which the Moroccan monarch wrote to King Philip III of France on this occasion. In it he invited the French King, in the name of kingly solidarity, to join in the operation to maintain royal authority against a rebellious son. It was this sentiment alone, he says, which permitted him to help a Castilian King towards whom he had so many causes for enmity. In the following year Alfonso X died and was succeeded by the son who had rebelled against him. Seeking to profit from the confusion in the Christian camp, the Moroccan ruler continued his campaign against the new King, crossing again in 1285. After some indecisive fighting he consented to make peace on condition that the Castilian King should not interfere in the affairs of Muslim Spain, that Muslim merchants should receive favourable treatment in Castilian territory, and that thirteen mule-loads of Arabic books which had been captured by the Christians on various occasions should be returned to Morocco where they were distributed among the libraries of the various student hostels. In return he promised to pay compensation for some of the damage done by his troops. After a period of peace, hostilities were resumed in 1339 by the formidable Abu al-Hassan who prepared a major onslaught on Castile. This was inaugurated by a brilliant naval victory in the Straits. The Muslim allies then besieged the Christians in Tarifa but were completely defeated by a Christian relief force on 30 October 1340. Though the Merinids continued to retain possession of Gibraltar until 1411 when they made it over to Granada (which lost it to the Castilians in 1463) and though they shared in guarding certain frontier fortresses, such as Ronda and Marbella, the battle of Tarifa was their last major intervention on Spanish soil. It took place 265 years after the original Moroccan intervention and 629 years after the Arab invasion.

For the remaining 152 years of the independence of Granada, that state never received anything more than fitful diplomatic aid from Morocco, and at one period Granada itself exerted a decisive influ/ ence on events in Fez.

The period of the Beni Merin and the Beni Wattas marked the final abandonment of Moroccan pretensions to authority in Spain and in the eastern Maghrib. A prolonged siege of Tlemsen from 1299 to 1307 failed to recover an area which was now the seat of a separate government; though later taken by Abu al-Hassan it was soon lost again. Having neither such a strong religious nor tribal basis as the Almoravids and the Almohads the Beni Merin began the creation of a state organization with a rudimentary civil service, largely Spanish Muslim in origin, and a rudimentary regular army. The latter consisted not only of Merinid cavalry but also of renegades as converted Christians were called by their fellow Europeans, of troops of Turkish origin, and of former Spanish Muslims.

Being northerners the Beni Merin transferred the capital from Marrakesh to Fez, a city which has henceforth been inseparably connected with their memory. In 1279 they constructed a new administrative city known as the White City or New Fez (Fez Jadid) on high ground above the old town. This contained the royal residence (as it does until today), barracks (qasbas) to shelter troops, government quarters, and a new Jewish quarter or mellah to which the Jews were transferred in order to be under the immediate pro/ tection of the ruler. This did not mean that the old city or medina was neglected. On the contrary the Beni Merin endowed it with many of its most famous and characteristic monuments, notably the madrasas. One of the finest of these is al-Attarin (1323–5) situated near the Qarawiyin mosque; another, higher up the town, is that of Bu Inaniya (1350–5). Such colleges consist of a central court, a basin for ablutions, a special court for prayers, and a number of small rooms which provided sleeping quarters for the students. High above the town on the north the later Merinids built monuments for their dead. These are now in ruins but are known to all visitors on account of the magnificent view of the city and surrounding country from the Moorish café situated beside them. Earlier members of the dynasty were buried in an enceinte which they constructed outside Rabat, known today as Chella; this is in relatively good preservation and with its gardens and its views is a favourite haunt for the people of Rabat to pass an idle hour. It was to emphasize the character of the early Beni Merin sovereigns as *mujahidun* or holy warriors that a site was chosen for their tombs near the city which formed the base for operations in Spain. Abu al-Hassan himself had the walls of the enclosure constructed in 1339. His son Abu Inan developed the site, which came to include two mosques and a hospice, and he devoted the proceeds from the New Bathhouse at Salé to its mainten-ance. It was here that he buried his mother, Shems ed-Duha (Morning Sun), a name which indicates that she had been a slave and no doubt a Christian. The inscription on her tombstone reads: Praise be to God! This is the grave of our lady, the noble, pure, devout, and saintly mother of the Sultan, Khalifa and Imam . . . our Lord, Commander of the Faithful, the reliant on the Lord of the Worlds, Abu Inan, son of the Commander of the Muslims, Abu al-Hassan . . . May God instal her in the fulness of his heaven and receive her with indulgence and pardon . . . Her death took place on the night preceding Saturday, the fourth of Rajab the unique, in the year 750, and she was buried after Friday prayer on the 25th day of the same month [8 October 1349], in the presence of our Khalifa, victorious by God's aid, and of principal personages of the East and the West who came in delegation to attend the interment. . . .

As can be seen from these lines Abu Inan adopted the title of Commander of the Faithful and the appelation of Caliph. He probably justified this by the fact that his father Abu al-Hassan had conquered the ruler of Tunis whose ancestor adopted the title of Caliph as heir of the Almohads at the moment when Al-Mamun rejected the claim of Ibn Tumart to be the Mahdi. From Abu Inan's time onward, most Moroccan rulers, though not regarded by outsiders as entitled to the title of Caliph, have generally been treated as having the attributes of Commanders of the Faithful within their own territories and have been described as Caliphs in their official communications.

The Beni Merin period marks a definite stage in the development of the Moroccan Makhzen or state organization and in the fixing of the frontiers by which the state has since been limited. The increased hostility towards Christians, due to the persecution and expulsion of the Muslims of Spain, is made clear by the fact that Christian European troops were no longer employed in Morocco but only renegades. In the artistic field the period marks the development of an aery grace and elegance in the construction of buildings and in their decoration. This takes the place of the 'austere and massive sobriety' of Almohad architecture; it was the age in which the artistic as well as the political and social forms of Andalusian life were most closely associated with those in Morocco. When Abu al-Hassan was about to marry a Tunisian princess, he decided to build a special palace for her. Having summoned masons, carpenters, mosaicists, marble workers, plumbers, painters, and iron and copper smiths, he told them:

I want a building with four rooms, each different, with two pavilions adjoining. The walls will have various types of decoration, in plasterwork and tiles. You will use cedar wood, carved and fitted, having floral and geometrical designs. The walls of the patio will be sculptured; it will be paved with marble and with tiles. There will be marble columns and basins. The architecture of each of the roofs will be different, suiting the methods of floral and polygonal decoration of the artisans; these ceilings will then be painted. The doors will be made of inlaid wood, as also the cupboards and the wicket-doors. Handles, locks, and other such decoration will be of polished and gilded copper or of plated iron.[7]

All this Abu al-Hassan wished to be carried out within one week. Unfortunately no Merinid palace has survived, but a good idea of the style can be formed from the decoration and disposition of the surviving madrasas and from the contemporary Alhambra palace at Granada. The setting of the latter is recalled by the ruins of the Merinid buildings at al-Mansura outside Tlemsen which were constructed during the seven years siege of the city. The beautiful site on an eminence, with the distant views of the plain, unmistakably recalls both Moroccan scenes and the Alhambra in Spain, though today Tlemsen lies in Algerian territory.

Though the three centuries of Merinid rule gave Morocco frontiers and a style of living and of architecture which it has never since lost, it brought also an increasing loss of creative power and a growing decadence. Christian invaders from the Iberian peninsula became ever more bold and it was during the rule of the Beni Merin that the Kingdom of Granada, the last remaining Muslim foothold in Spain, was finally overwhelmed in 1492 without any attempt being made from Morocco to avert the catastrophe.

One incidental result of the fall of that city was that a Muslim boy, named Hassan ibn Muhammad, born in Granada two years after its fall, emigrated to Fez to pursue his studies. In 1513 he visited Timbuctu and Lake Chad. In following years he travelled to Constantinople and then through Arabia, Armenia, and Persia, finally reaching Egypt and travelling up the Nile as far as Assuan. On his way home by sea he was captured by privateers, probably Sicilian or Maltese, off the island of Jerba. His knowledge and intelligence led his captors to present him to Pope Leo, instead of selling him in the slave markets of Pisa or Genoa. He was induced to adopt the Christian faith, received the names of John Leo and a pension from his patron the Pope, learned Latin from a Cardinal, acquired Italian, and gave lessons in Arabic. Under the name Leo Africanus he wrote a *Description of Africa* which long remained the principal authority on the subject. About 1552 he left Rome for Tunis where he soon afterwards died, having reverted, it is said, to his ancestral faith.

30   The unfinished tower of the Hassan mosque at Rabat was built during the
period of the Almohad caliphate in the twelfth century.

31 and 32 The strength of the Almo-
had movement was the achievement of a
Berber religious reformer Ibn Tumart.
The Kutubia mosque (*below*) at
Marrakesh and the tower of the Almohad
mosque, now the cathedral at Giralda in
Seville (*left*), date from this period.

33 A close link had already developed with Muslim Spain and the Almoravids had encountered the greatest monument of Moorish art – the Mezquita at Cordoba in Seville which dates from the eighth century.

34 The Almohad régime collapsed in 1268, and was succeeded by the Beni Marin or Merinids who endeavoured to restore the Muslim position in Spain but without success. The palace at Alhambra in Granada dates from this period.

35 The Merinid Sultan Abu al-Hassan (1330-51) built the necropolis at Chella in Rabat where his remains and those of his family are buried.

36 After the period of anarchy in the sixteenth century, Morocco was reunited by the Saadian dynasty. The tombs of the Saadian leaders at Marrakesh date from this period.

37 This page from the Quran written in 1568 entitled the 'Chapter of Victory' shows the characteristic Maghribi Script which is different from that of the East.

38 A sanctuary of a Muslim holy man. The *murábits* who assumed leadership after the Saadian collapse made use of such sanctuaries to establish political power.

39 The *murábits* were overthrown in 1688 by the Alawite dynasty. This gate at Meknès which became the Moroccan capital dates from this period.

40 Ramparts were built to defend the Moroccan cities taken over by the Portuguese during the fifteenth and sixteenth centuries. The city of Al-Jadida (Mazagan) dates from this period.

41 The Portuguese also built magnificent vaulted cisterns such as this one also at Al-Jadida (Mazagan).

42 Tangier was captured by the Portuguese in 1471 as this contemporary tapestry by Nuno Gonçalves illustrates.

43 The Saadian Sultan Ahmad al-Mansur made trade agreements with England in the sixteenth century. This is a letter he wrote to Elizabeth I.

44 Caid ben Abdalla was Moroccan ambassador to Charles I of England.

45 Sallee Rovers known as corsairs were Morisco refugees from Spain and tried to make a treaty with Charles I. This plan dated 1637 shows the English fleet at the Port of Salé.

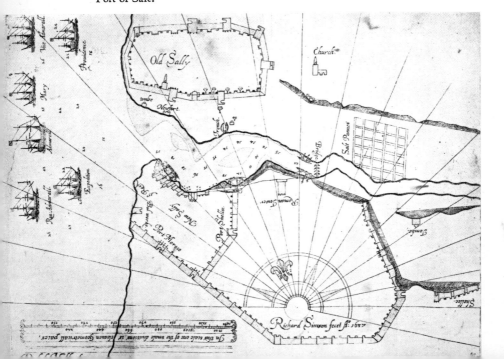

5   Collapse and recovery

WE NOW ENTER A PHASE of Moroccan history of which the main feature is the successful Moroccan reaction to the Christian invasion of their shores.

Spanish raids on Moroccan ports began more than two hundred years before the fall of Granada. In 1260, shortly after the conquest of Cordoba and Seville, the Spaniards assembled much shipping in the harbour of Salé, ostensibly to deliver arms to a pretender to the Moroccan throne. They then took the opportunity to seize the town while the inhabitants were celebrating the Id al Kebir. They held it for fourteen days till they were driven out by the Merinid, Abu Yusuf Yaacub. One hundred and forty years later, in 1400, a Spanish force made a surprise landing near Tetuan which captured and destroyed the city, massacring half the citizens and enslaving the rest. In the course of the fifteenth century the Spaniards also raided the Atlantic coast constantly, attacking among other places Azem-mour, Mamora, and Fedala, 'killing, enslaving, and robbing'. In 1485 this led the Wattasid ruler of Fez to protest to the Catholic kings. These attacks could perhaps be defended as by-products of the reconquest. Portugal, however, which had recovered all her territory by about 1260, had no such justification for her unprovoked onslaught on Ceuta in 1415. This is generally described by English and French (though not by Portuguese) writers as a 'reprisal for Moorish piracy'. In fact Muslims expelled from Spain did raid the northern shores of the Straits and also attack Spanish shipping. Portuguese trade however seems not to have been seriously molested;

indeed the Portuguese King, John I, opposed the suggested attack on Ceuta on the grounds that it would be sure to provoke reprisals against Portuguese shipping in the Straits and so imperil the valuable Portuguese trade in oil and wine with the Mediterranean ports. He would himself have preferred a joint attack with the Castilians against Granada, from which Portugal might have won territory and so strengthen herself with respect to Castile. The initiative for the attack came from the King's half-English sons by his wife, Philippa of Lancaster; their motives appear to have been in part ambition and in part the desire to find an outlet for unemployed adventurers left idle by the conclusion of peace with Castile. They hoped to win control of the Straits and later to capture Fez. It was an extension to overseas of the half religious and half worldy instinct which had led to the policy of steadily dominating the Muslims in the Peninsula, achieved in Portugal 150 years earlier but still continuing in Spain. At the time of the Portuguese recapture of Lisbon, in 1147, the Muslim governor of the city in his reply to the ultimatum delivered to him by the Archbishop of Braga had stigmatized it as ambition. 'I never cease to marvel at you people,' he said. 'While any amount of lions or elephants are satisfied with one wood or district, neither land nor sea can contain you, since you are actuated not by necessity but by ambition.'[8] When King John finally gave his consent to the attack on Ceuta he insisted, against his Queen's prayers, in participating in person in spite of his age in the hope he said that by now shedding the blood of infidels he could atone for the Christian blood which he had shed in the past. The city was duly captured and sacked and the inhabitants enslaved. Twelve years later when the King's successor attacked Tangier, the expedition proved disastrous and his brother Ferdinand had to be surrendered as guarantee that Ceuta would be handed back to the Muslims in return for their allowing the Portuguese army to re-embark for Portugal. Having recovered his army, the King refused to hand Ceuta over, in spite of the imprisoned Prince's entreaties that he should. Retained in captivity and ill-treated the Prince died in Fez six years later. The episode is the theme of Calderon's play *El Principe Constante*.

Undiscouraged by this setback, the Portuguese in the course of the next fifty years, gained possession of almost every port on the Straits and on the Atlantic coast. Only Salé and Badis (near Peñon de Vélez), both of which were frequented by Venetian and Genoese shipping, remained in Moroccan possession. The first to go was Alcazarseghir between Tangier and Ceuta (1452), followed by Arzila and Tangier (1471). Between 1496 and 1508 Massa south of Agadir, and then Agadir itself, were acquired; and then Mazagan, Mogador, and Safi, until finally a protectorate, with Safi as capital, was established over the whole neighbouring region of Dukkala. The Moroccans in the protected areas were known as *mouros de pazes* (well-disposed or peaceful Muslims). Soon however difficulties began to arise. In Morocco there was a ferment of feeling which was to give rise ultimately to the reunification of the country under the Saadian dynasty, while in Portugal there was an intensification of the crusading spirit, perhaps stimulated by the Spanish capture of Granada. Thus in Azemmour, which had accepted Portuguese protection in 1486, relations began to become strained from about 1502; when there was no improvement by 1508 the Portuguese king decided to seize the city by force. A first attempt in 1509 failed, but a second in 1513 proved successful. Patriotic feeling was stirred by an exhortation specially composed for the occasion by the great poet and dramatist, Gil Vicente. This contained the lines:

> *The King of Fez is fainting,*
> *Marrakesh gives loud cries.*
> *For Africa was Christian;*
> *The Muslims robbed you of it . . .*
> *But now His Majesty determines*
> *To magnify the faith,*
> *By making mosque cathedral,*
> *By grace divine, in Fez.*
> *For war, yes, war unceasing*
> *Is now his great intent.*

In the King's mind the capture of Azemmour was to be the prelude to the capture of Marrakesh. In fact however it marked the beginning of the rapid decay of Portuguese influence. This was in part due to the diversion of Portuguese interest to other spheres, but was promoted also by the hostility aroused by the attack. The Muslim inhabitants of Azemmour abandoned their city; their example was followed by neighbouring towns and the countryside was deserted so that Azemmour had to be provisioned from outside. The ruler in Fez, hitherto too occupied with civil dissension to interfere, now moved to attack and though this had no effect on the city it caused the 'well-disposed Moors' in general to become disaffected.

Meanwhile, increasing Spanish successes in the campaigns against the Kingdom of Granada, combined with the growing menace of the Turkish advance, led Spain to carry the war into Africa. Her chief effort was in the east since she had undertaken, by a number of agreements, of which the Treaty of Tordesillas in 1494 is the best known, to regard the Kingdom of Fez as a Portuguese reserve, as far as the occupation of territory was concerned. This however did not debar her in 1497 from occupying Melilla on the grounds that it was part of the Kingdom of Tlemsen not of Fez; nor did it prevent her from seizing the Peñon de Vélez Gomara in 1508 on the flimsy pretext that it was a separate princedom. These encroachments naturally raised intense indignation in Morocco, not only against the foreigners but also against the Muslim rulers who were unable to defend the country. On this occasion no tribal leader appeared to take charge. Leadership began to pass to two distinct types of people, in each case on account of the virtue attributed to them as men of religion. One type was the *murábit* (marabout) whose power was derived from asceticism or other religious observances. These tended to belong to mystic orders which had long taken root in Morocco. The second type were members of Sherifian families whose prestige like that of the Idrisids was derived from a combination of descent from the Prophet with a reputation for virtue and practical ability. One such Sherifian family, or reputed such, were the Beni Saad, settled south of the Atlas. It was said that they had been invited, years before, to come from Arabia and settle in the Sous in order that their blessed presence might have a beneficial effect on the date crop. Members of this family now began to take the lead in organizing resistance to the Portuguese and took advantage of the collapse of the Beni Merin and the Beni Wattas to establish independent kingdoms in Tarudant and Marrakesh. This had the result that from soon after 1500 Morocco was regarded in Europe as two separate kingdoms, Fez and Morocco – the latter word being simply a Europeanized form of the name Marrakesh. The history of the struggles between the last sovereigns of the Beni Wattas and the Saadians and between various members of the Saadian family themselves are highly complicated. It is enough to know that Saadian leaders recovered many ports in south Morocco from the Christians and in the end established their rule over the whole country.

In the south where the Portuguese came into conflict with the Saadian Sherifs their principal base was Agadir, known to them as Santa Cruz de Aguer. We have a vivid account of life there written by one of the garrison who became a prisoner of the Moroccans when they captured the settlement in 1541.[9] From this we see how intolerable these Christian posts must have been for the inhabitants, but also how relatively prosperous this area of Morocco previously seems to have been. The author for example tells how a Portuguese raiding party hid one night outside a town called Azro. When the sun was up, the gates open, and the cattle coming out, they made a surprise attack, killed a number of people in the gate, broke into the town and returned with much booty – Muslim slaves, boys and girls, merchandise of all sorts, garments, horses, mules, wheat, barley, dates, almonds, and other fruits, much of which they found ready loaded on camels. The writer adds that presently no settlement remained in the neighbourhood which had not been thus sacked. In consequence the humblest Portuguese in the settlement was prosperous and well supplied with slaves of both sexes. The Muslims who co-operated with them were equally well off, though as they would not hold Muslim slaves their share of the booty was entirely in kind.

The brutality of this kind of warfare was the common currency of the time. When later we hear of Moroccan ships from Salé raiding the south coast of England, it is to be remembered that such raids were belated reprisals for a century of Christian raiding on the Moroccan coast.

Unnecessary cruelty seems however to have been avoided and captives were generally ransomed, sooner or later. The Portuguese writer was for example shocked at the behaviour of some Canary Islanders, presumably Spaniards, who had been invited to help the garrison. 'The men of the Canaries', he says, 'wrought great and terrible cruelties, snatching children from their mothers' arms, one taking one leg and one the other, and cutting them in two with their swords up to their heads.' The writer seems to have been genuinely shocked, apart from the consideration which he mentions that such behaviour would provoke reprisals in kind. There are in fact indications that in other respects the same sort of friendly relations existed at times between the Moroccans and the Portuguese as existed later between them and their other 'protectors'. There are for example accounts of the ladies of the Portuguese garrison being invited to villages to watch powder-play and Portuguese doctors were often invited to treat Moroccan patients.

Portuguese occupation of Moroccan territory reached its greatest extension in the first quarter of the sixteenth century. In 1517 their position was weakened by the death of Fernandez Ataide their most experienced leader and two years later by the death of Yahya ibn Tafoufa their most trustworthy Moroccan ally. The fall of Agadir in 1541 marked a turning-point. By now Portugal had far greater interests elsewhere overseas; and having lost Agadir she evacuated Mogador, Safi, and Azemmour. Of all her possessions in the south she retained only Mazagan which for prestige reasons was not surrendered until 1769. Until today, there remain at Mazagan interesting Portuguese constructions including a magnificent vaulted cistern.

Meanwhile a new factor was making itself felt. This was the power of the Ottoman Turks whose fleets and corsairs won for them possession of all North Africa east of Morocco between the first and third quarters of the sixteenth century. Naturally these adventurers thought of pushing on into Morocco. One of the last Beni Wattas rulers in Fez actually did homage to the Ottoman Sultan and in 1553 it was with the aid of Turkish troops from Algiers that he re-established himself for a few months only in Fez.

Twenty-three years later, when Saadian princes were disputing the northern kingdom, a Saadian claimant to the throne, by name Abd al-Malik, with his mother and his brother Ahmad, took refuge in Constantinople. Through his stay there he acquired a largely Turkish outlook and in 1576 he also established himself in Fez with the aid of Turkish troops from Algiers. For a very brief period prayer seems to have been said in the name of the Ottoman Caliph. Once firmly on the throne, however, Abd al-Malik paid off the Turkish troops and rejected any sort of subjection to Turkish political supremacy.

The Turks had arrived in the eastern Maghrib invited by the local Arab leaders to assist in driving out the Spaniards. This result was achieved but the Arabs found that they had got rid of Spanish rule only to come under Turkish. The rulers of Morocco were determined that the same fate should not befall themselves and as the Spaniards were debarred by their agreement with Portugal from acquiring possessions in Morocco the Saadian ruling princes found it convenient to use them as a counterweight to the Turks. Unsuccessful pretenders or displaced sovereigns were on the other hand ready to seek Turkish help, as we have seen in Abd al-Malik's case, or to look farther afield to other European powers. For the moment Saadian-Spanish co-operation had unfortunate results for the last remnants of the Muslims of Granada. When these revolted, some years after the fall of Granada, they naturally looked to the Saadian ruler of Fez, then Maulay Abdullah, brother and predecessor of Abd al-Malik, for aid. This he would have liked to give but he had no ships to transport troops nor dared he ally himself with his Turkish enemies. All he could do was to permit arms smuggling and find work as settlers or soldiers for those who escaped.

The middle of the sixteenth century was a time when Moroccan diplomacy was very active in Europe and there were many attempted combinations between Moroccan and European rulers. Maulay Abdullah, for example, had tried a few years earlier to secure troops from the French King. This he proposed to pay for by the cession of Alcazarseghir, a small port to the east of Tangier.

Such negotiations with the infidels were much disliked by the religious leaders and the people. Thus Maulay Abdullah, who was personally pious and described by an eminent *murábit* as not a sultan but a saint, was deeply suspect to others. When he died, these verses were put on his tomb.

> *O you who visit my grave, pray for me generously, for I have need of it.*
> *Once the command of the faithful and the royalty was mine and my fame*
> *was great in the land.*
> *Now here I lie cast in this pit where no minister nor caid avails me.*
> *But I believed in God, my merciful judge, and my provision of faith was*
> *great.*
> *One who like me believes in His heaven has cause to hope for His pardon,*
> *For God in His goodness has said that what His servant believes of Him*
> *He will fulfil.*[10]

It was probably indignation at his failure to help the Muslims of Granada that caused his son to suspect the writer of these lines of malice. 'When you wrote "this pit",' he said, 'you must have been thinking of the tradition of the Prophet, "The grave is a garden of Paradise; the pit, a pit of Hell." You should have put "this ditch" or something like that.'

The extension of political relations with Europe was matched by an increase in commercial dealings. There was an active trade with the Netherlands and with England and a considerable number of European merchants settled in Marrakesh. In 1577 Abd al-Malik proposed to Queen Elizabeth a political alliance against Spain and a trade agreement. Queen Elizabeth sent an ambassador, Edmund Hogan, to Morocco and a trade agreement was made though no political alliance. The first reference to such trade dates from nearly twenty-five years earlier when a 'tall ship, called the *Lion*, of London, of about 150 tunnes' sailed 'for traffique into the Kingdom of Marocco in Barbarie', taking with it linen, woollens, cloth, coral, amber, and jet and bringing back sugar, dates, almonds, and 'malassos or sugar syroppe'. English sailors were held to be the most experienced in the Agadir and Safi coast and were employed as pilots, 'merchant-wise', by the Netherlands merchants. In 1585 a Barbary Company was formed for trade with Morocco.

While Abd al-Malik was conducting these negotiations his

dispossessed nephew Maulay Muhammad was seeking aid abroad. The only place where he received encouragement was Lisbon. Here the young King Sebastian was filled with a crusading spirit and dreamed of restoring the Portuguese position in Morocco. Maulay Muhammad therefore agreed to recognize Sebastian as his suzereign if he should regain his throne with Portuguese aid; he would also make over to Portugal the port of Arzila, which was in the possession of his followers. King Sebastian in July 1578 accordingly sailed with a force of Portuguese, of German mercenaries, and of Papal troops under the Englishman Thomas Stukeley who was taking them to head a rising in Ireland but had been driven by adverse winds into Lisbon.

Abd al-Malik, who had a valuable second in his brother, Ahmad, was by now firmly established in Morocco. He wore Turkish dress, put his soldiers into Turkish uniforms, and taught them Turkish military methods. He was European-minded also, spoke Spanish and some Italian, and had a knowledge of the Old and the New Testaments. He employed English musicians and is the only Moroccan ruler known to have signed his name on an official document in the Latin alphabet. Queen Elizabeth's ambassador, Edmund Hogan, used to accompany him bull-baiting with English dogs.

Having disembarked at Arzila, Sebastian decided to march on Larache in spite of the blazing heat and the certainty of getting out of touch with the fleet. The army was incredibly encumbered with wives and children, with several hundred priests, including the Papal Nuncio and a number of bishops, with camp followers and with a number of gilded coaches in which the King and his notables were to make the journey. Having left 1,000 men in Arzila, the King reviewing his army found, in the words of the contemporary English dramatist, George Peele, that

> . . . he had two thousand arméd horses
> And fourteen thousand men that serve on foot,
> Three hundred pioneers and a thousand coachmen,
> Besides a number almost numberless
> Of drudges, negro-slaves, and muleteers,

Horse-boies, laundresses, and courtisans,
And fifteen hundred wagons full of stuffe
For noblemen brought up in delicate.[11]

He also however had a considerable force of artillery and the army was formidable enough to lead Abd al-Malik, who was himself now suffering from a mortal illness, to offer extremely favourable terms. Obsessed by the desire for glory Sebastian refused. Abd al-Malik thereupon launched his attack when the Portuguese army, exhausted with the heat and several days march, was in the neighbourhood of Alcazarquivir. The Portuguese fought in a square, with women and children, camp followers and coaches in the centre. The result was their total defeat, with the loss of 26,000 persons captured or killed. The pretender, Maulay Muhammad, was drowned in a river while fleeing. Sebastian was killed, and Abd al-Malik died of his illness, early in the battle, after marshalling his troops in a supreme effort. The battle is known as the battle of Alcazarquivir, of the Three Kings, or of the Wadi Makhazin from the river in which the Moroccan pretender was drowned. It was popularly believed that during the battle a famous Moroccan saint, Sidi Abu al-Abbas al-Sibti had appeared to the Muslim army. Mounted on a grey horse he was seen going from side to side, encouraging the combatants. 'Such things', says the Moroccan historian, al-Ifrani, who describes the battle, 'are not to be disbelieved, for it is known that the martyrs are ever living in God's presence.'

The victory, the vast booty, and the ransom for the prisoners brought a great accession to the prestige and wealth of the Saadian dynasty. In Europe, Morocco began to be taken seriously as a potential contemporary power.

The death of Sultan Abd al-Malik might nevertheless have ruined everything. In fact, however, the succession passed on the field of battle without any disturbance to Ahmad, the late Sultan's brother, who took the title of *al-Mansur* (the Victorious). For Portugal, on the contrary, the death of King Sebastian was disastrous. He had no children and the crown within a few months passed to Philip of Spain, inaugurating what the Portuguese call 'the Spanish captivity' which lasted from 1580 to 1640. This was a misfortune for

Morocco also, since the much more powerful Spain now inherited Ceuta, which it has retained ever since, and became free to occupy Moroccan ports on the Atlantic.

Like his brother, Sultan Ahmad was alert to the ideas and politics of Europe. He also was a good Arabic scholar, collected a great library, and enjoyed composing the type of verse, full of artificial conceits, which appeals to Arab but not to European taste.

The Saadian régime had no tribal basis. Ahmad therefore constituted a regular mercenary army, amounting in all to about 40,000. The majority of these were Turks, that is men from the Ottoman domains. There was also a force of 4,000 so-called renegades, men of Christian origin who for one reason or another had adopted the Muslim faith. Another corps of 4,000 men consisted of Muslim refugees from Spain; another, of 1,500 Algerian Berbers, was recruited from the Kabyle tribe which later gave its name to the French Zouaves. The Sultan could also call on tribal contingents which then, as later, were not very dependable.

The new Sultan maintained the diplomatic and trade relations already initiated with various European states and particularly with England. English merchants wished to sell cloth, and to buy sugar which was made from the cane introduced into the Sous at least as early as 1154 when it is mentioned by al-Idrisi. Queen Elizabeth's household is recorded to have consumed 18,000 lb. of Moroccan sugar in the course of one year. Another Moroccan product, salt-petre, was much sought after for military purposes, while the Sultan was equally anxious to acquire English arms, and wood and ship-building materials in general. The latter exchanges gave rise to diplomatic protests since Christian sentiment in Europe regarded the sale of war materials to Muslims as a form of apostasy, while in Morocco there was a similar objection to the sale of war materials to Christian states. These exchanges had therefore to be carried on surreptitiously, though they seem to have had the acquiescence and indeed encouragement of the two governments.

The Dutch, like the English, were hostile to Spain, and also built up active commercial relations with Morocco. They were greatly assisted in this by Jewish refugees from Spain who had settled in Holland while maintaining good relations with their co-religion-ists in Morocco.

Sultan Ahmad was an ambitious ruler. Finding his way to the east blocked by the Turks, he was moved by the dream of restoring Moroccan influence in Spain. Here he thought of Queen Elizabeth as a possible ally and was much encouraged when she sanctioned the sale to him of 600 tons of Sussex timber. In 1587, with the Spanish threat to England imminent, he suggested that the Queen should send him 100 English ships to transport Moroccan troops to Spain, offering to pay 150,000 ducats as soon as the ships arrived at a Moroccan port. This project was not accepted; but in the following year the Moroccan authorities had to restore order in Marrakesh when the defeat of the Spanish Armada provoked a riot between English and Spanish merchants living there.

Unable to expand to the north any more than to the east, Sultan Ahmad now turned his attention to the south. In 1581 he had made an expedition to the oases of Gourara and Tuat in the central Sahara, as the result of which he controlled the output of salt from the neighbouring mines which was traded for the gold of west Africa. The Sudanese rulers then proceeded to exploit other mines farther south. On the pretext that he needed the money for the Holy War, Ahmad now demanded from the Negro ruler of Songhai a tribute on each load of salt extracted and exported. When the ultimatum was rejected the Sultan sent an expedition of 4,000 men, of whom 1,500 were Arab lancers and the remainder mainly Spanish Muslim refugees, or renegades, armed with arquebuses. The march across the desert was terrible; the expedition which took the route through Tinduf, Taghaza, and Taoudeni, lost half its effec-tives before it reached the Niger, 135 days later. On 13 March 1591 the black army, like that of the Mahdi 300 years later at Omdurman, could do nothing against the firearms of the whites and was com-pletely defeated. The Moroccan commander Jouder, who came from the Granada district of Spain, forwarded to the Sultan an offer from the Songhai King of an indemnity of 100,000 pieces of gold and 10,000 slaves, to be followed by an annual tribute and the monopoly of the salt trade. Ahmad rejected the offer and replaced

Pasha Jouder by another named Mahmud who occupied the whole country.

The victory was celebrated in a lengthy poem which begins:

The army of the dawn charged the darkness of the night
And the oncoming white extinguished the black.

This victory resulted in a further great increase of prestige and of wealth, and brought Sultan Ahmad the title of *al-Dhahabi* (the Golden), in addition to *al-Mansur* (the Victorious). Apart from gold and slaves, the first returning convoy brought civet and civet-cats, ebony, rhinoceros horns, horses, eunuchs, dwarfs, and thirteen virgin daughters of the King of Gao. The conquered area was governed from Timbuctu for forty-two years as a protectorate under Pashas sent from Morocco. After this the Pashas became virtually independent rulers, though there were periodical reassertions of Moroccan supremacy. In 1780 their title was changed to Kahya; this régime continued until the arrival of the French in 1893.

The French orientalist Houdas who studied this period wrote:

If the Moroccan conquest had certain deplorable results in the Sudan it would be unjust to deny that it exerted a favourable influence at one time. As long as the Pashas were appointed by the Moroccan emperor and had a financial control beside them, the situation of the Sudanese was happier than it had been. Trade was more flourishing and the relations between the banks of the Niger and the shores of the Mediterranean became more important and frequent. The spread of Islam brought about a perceptible improvement by restraining slavery to some extent, since no free-born Muslim could be enslaved.[12]

It was during the Moroccan period that the only two important chronicles of the country were composed by its Negro inhabitants.

Timbuctu had, however, already been a centre of Muslim learning, and when a rising occurred three years after the capture of the country Ahmad Baba, a famous black scholar, was made prisoner and brought in fetters to Marrakesh. During the journey the chains caused him to fall from his camel and break his leg. It was not till two years later that he was released from confinement and permitted to lecture to a highly appreciative audience in Marrakesh. He was received by al-Mansur who was holding audience from behind a screen. 'God, be he exalted,' exclaimed the Sheikh in indignation;

'has said in the Quran that man can only be addressed by God through revelation or from behind a screen. I see that you take God as your model, but if you wish to converse with me, draw the veil and come near.' When the Sultan did so, Ahmad Baba asked for what reason his house had been sacked, his library dispersed, and himself brought to Marrakesh in chains, so that he fell from his camel and broke his leg. 'Our purpose', the Sultan replied, 'was to unite the Muslim world. As you were one of the most distinguished Muslims of your country, your submission would help to bring about that of your compatriots.' 'If that was your purpose,' said the Sheikh, 'why could you not have begun with the Turks at Tlemsen, and other places much nearer to you than we were?' Ahmad Baba had to wait till al-Mansur's death seven years later before he was permitted by his successor to go home. In the meanwhile he addressed his compatriots in verse:

> O you who travel to Kaghu, turn aside to my village.
> Whisper my name to my friends and convey to them
> A sweet-scented greeting from an exile, homesick
> For his country, his kindred, and his friends and neighbours.[13]

Fortified with his victory and enriched by the spoil, al-Mansur renewed the proposal to the English government for a political alliance against Spain. Queen Elizabeth's advisers would, earlier, have been glad of Moroccan aid in landing English troops in Portugal in order to support a pretender against Philip II, who had now become King of Portugal as well as of Spain; later they would have welcomed Moroccan financial aid in an assault on the Spanish possessions in America. But al-Mansur was interested only in an attack on south Spain, which Elizabeth did not want. In 1596 when an Anglo-Dutch force captured Cadiz, the Dutch proposed that the city should be handed over to al-Mansur, and it was decided 'to send Sir Edward Hoby to the King of Morocco for galleys, men, and victuals as occasion required', but this was cancelled next day. The only Muslim participation seems to have been the action of a Moorish slave who blew up the *St Philip*, the Spanish admiral, a ship of 1,500 tons, by setting fire to the gunpowder, incidentally destroying also two or three nearby ships. In 1600 al-Mansur had no intention of helping English operations in America without a clear understanding what Morocco was to get out of this. However three Moroccan ambassadors proceeded to London. Merchants who traded with Morocco were active in trying to secure a courteous welcome for them. The government listened, did not commit themselves, but promised to send an ambassador to Marrakesh who would carry a verbal message, the matter being too weighty, it was told them, to entrust to paper. The city merchants as a whole were suspicious. They recognized that the ambassadors had delivered to the Queen a number of captive Netherlanders whose release she had been anxious to secure; but it was held that their main purpose was commercial intelligence and that they had come to find out for how much Moroccan sugar was sold and to see whether they could raise their price for it. Others were shocked by their Muslim religion and their habits, remarking how they killed all their meat, sheep, and chickens, within the premises where they were lodged, and turned to the east to do so; and how they used rosaries and prayed (it was said) to saints. Their request to be sent on to the Levant in an English ship was denounced as a thing which, if granted, would be a mark of friendliness and familiarity with infidels which would be scandalous in the eyes of the world. The eldest and most pious member of the party, Si al-Hajj Massa, died on the eve of their departure. 'The Barbarians' (i.e. the men from Barbary), said one of these ill-disposed merchants, 'were at court yesterday and will be gone shortly; but the eldest of them, who was a kind of priest or prophet, hath taken his leave of the world and is gone to prophecy *apud inferos* and to seek out Mahound their mediator.'

This was the last Moroccan approach to Elizabethan England. Three years later the English lost their Virgin Queen and the Moroccans their Golden Sultan.

In England the death of the Queen brought about the union of two parts of the British Isles into one kingdom; in Morocco the death of the Sultan meant that the throne was disputed among three sons, none of them worthy, and that the realm was once again divided into a Kingdom of Fez and a Kingdom of Marrakesh. Nominally, Saadian rule continued in Fez until 1628 and in Marrakesh until

1659, but it was a period of dreary internecine strife, tedious to record. An Englishman, Captain John Smith, later famous in Virginia, who had thought to take service under al-Mansur's son, Maulay Zidan, of Marrakesh, left again having found 'perfidious, treacherous and bloody murders rather than war'. Maulay Zidan (1604–27) had indeed indomitable courage which enabled him three times to regain the throne from which he had been deposed. Like his father he was a man of letters and something of a poet. Seeing a tomb one day, he was moved to improvise:

> 'I passed by a tomb in a garden, gay with flowers.
> "Whose is it?" I asked. "Hush," they said,
> With a gesture of pity, "A lover is buried here."'

Other evidence of Maulay Zidan's interest in literature is given by his distress at the loss of 3,000 Arabic manuscripts and books, mostly from al-Mansur's library. Despatched by sea in a French ship from Safi to Agadir they were captured by Spanish ships and declared a legitimate prize by a Spanish court at Cadiz. Lengthy negotiations with Philip III of Spain failed, on account of that King's excessive demands. The manuscripts were deposited in the Escorial where a great part were destroyed by the fire which raged there for fifteen days in 1671 while the remainder form the basis of the existing great collection. The loss of Arabic books in Spain was a constant pre-occupation of Arab scholars of the period. 'The Great Mosque at Cordoba', wrote a Muslim historian, 'is filled with books but the doors are shut. It has become the dwelling of insects and the haunt of dogs.' An Arab writer of the sixteenth century, describing what he had heard of al-Andalus under Christian rule, adds that these books were removed from the Mezquita when the Christian Cathedral was constructed inside it in 1523. They were then, he says, transferred to a building opposite, of which the door was kept locked. 'And a Spaniard told me in 1573', he adds, 'that if you put your ear to the door, you can actually hear the worms munching the documents.'

When the Saadians first appeared in Fez they appeared to the citizens as primitive people from the south, wearing garments which looked like brightly-coloured bedspreads. But they possessed the same power of adaptation as the dynasties which preceded them and their lack of refinement was soon remedied. In this they were much assisted by two court officials whom they took over from the Beni Merin. One, a man named Qasim al-Zerhouni, showed them what clothes to wear and how to put them on. He taught them how to roll their turbans, how to harness their horses, and how to behave in company. He settled questions of precedence for them, explained the way to issue orders and the manner of consulting with high officials and of talking with men of letters. He taught them when and how to eat, and how to serve food to guests. The other, a woman, the house-keeper bint Najjou, showed the women how food should be prepared, how meals should be spaced through the day, according to the season. She indicated to them appropriate sauces and dainties, and the personnel necessary. She gave them hints on the art of dressing, on the use of perfumes, and on what clothes would be suitable on great occasions. She showed them the use to be made of silk coverlets and of embroidery for pillows and curtains. In short, while al-Zerhouni saw to the external splendour of the Saadian household, she made its internal elegance her affair.

In the sphere of art, the Saadians continued to develop the Spanish Muslim forms initiated by the Beni Merin. The chief novelty which they introduced was the use of Italian marble in large quantities, often worked by Italian craftsmen. The greatest construction of Ahmad al-Mansur was his palace in Marrakesh, called al-Badia (the Peerless). As the poet said:

> The care of kings who wish their memory to live is to speak with the
> tongues of buildings;
> For if the building bear the sign of greatness, it proves the greatness of
> its maker.[14]

We have descriptions of al-Badia, but these do not enable us to know how we should have judged it. It received much praise from the panegyrists:

> No palace but is put to shame by al-Badia.
> Within ripe fruits and flowers distill their fragrance.
> The perfumed soil, the glorious prospect, the cool waters and the lofty
> towers

Which climb time's summits, are the glory of Marrakesh and its pride.[14]
But al-Mansur did not only hear flattery on the subject of his
palace. He one day asked one of those holy simpletons who haunt
the east for his opinion of it. 'Well, master,' replied the Fool, 'it'll
make a big heap of rubble when it's demolished.' The palace was in
fact destroyed and its rich materials carried away by a ruler of the
succeeding dynasty within three-quarters of a century. What remains
today is a great shell of crumbling walls, against which the apartments once rested. In the centre is an ornamental pool surrounded
with sunken orange orchards which still perfume the air. In this
state the Badia today provides an incomparable setting for the festival
of Berber folk dancing organized by the energetic Minister of
Tourism, Maulay Ahmed Alawi, every spring.

6   Collapse and withdrawal

THE COLLAPSE OF THE SAADIAN DYNASTY involved the
renewed division of Morocco into two and, for a time into four
princedoms – Fez, Marrakesh, Tarudant, and Tafilalet. In addition
a tiny independent state came into being in the Anti-Atlas with its
capital at Iligh (Tazerwalt). The division was accompanied by,
and in part was the result of, a revival of the popular religious and
national ferment to which earlier Saadian successes had afforded a
more orderly outlet. Leadership was assumed by a number of
individual *murábits* or holy men, and by one *zawiya*, an institution
best described as a non-celibate monastery. Eventually it was a
Sherifian family of Tafilalet which won the throne for themselves,
but in the meantime other leaders made and unmade the official
rulers of the country, acted as more or less authentic voices of the
national conscience, and in cases acquired such influence as to
appear themselves possible candidates for supreme power. One of
these, Abu Mahalli, whom English writers (now in fairly close
touch with Morocco through the trade connexions) refer to as 'Bum
Hully', first established himself in Tafilalet and then gradually
extended his power to Marrakesh. Developing political ambitions
he was for a time successful in expelling al-Mansur's son, Maulay
Zidan. He was then overthrown by a rival murábit from the Atlas
who in his turn succumbed to Maulay Zidan, who thus recovered
his capital. Another, al-Samlali, originating in the Agadir area,
got control of both Tarudant and Tafilalet; his son remained in
possession of parts of the Sous and of the Anti-Atlas until 1670.
Another, al-Masnawi, became virtually independent as ruler of

Gourara and Tuat in the central Sahara. In the Straits area Ghailan, known to the English as Gayland, was more of a holy warrior than saint. When the English in 1662 became possessed of Tangier, on the marriage of the Portuguese princess Catharine of Braganza to Charles II, Ghailan was their principal enemy until he became an ally when threatened by the murábits of Dila and by the new dynasty. For some time another murábit, al-Ayyashi, was also a competitor for supremacy in the area between Tangier and Larache. Al-Ayyashi operated chiefly against the Spaniards installed at Larache since 1610 and was described to James I as 'the great Murábit or Saint who commandeth all that part of Barbary towards the Straits'.

The zawiya of Dila, near Khénifra in the Middle Atlas, was founded about 1600 and in time it came to control the greater part of northern Morocco, including Fez, Meknès, and the plain towards Rabat. As its reputation increased, the murábits became increasingly worldly and aspired to political power. Their influence came to an end after three-quarters of a century, when the zawiya was destroyed by the first ruler of the Alawite dynasty, Maulay al-Rashid, in 1668.

In the Morocco of this time there was yet another element which for a while acquired a power of independent action. These were Morisco refugees from Spain. They were remnants of the Spanish Muslims who had been nominally converted to Christianity and now did not really know to what faith they belonged or to what nation. Some of them settled in Tetuan joining earlier Spanish Muslim refugees who had rebuilt the city about 1500, just a hundred years after its destruction by the Spanish.

A larger number settled at Rabat. One group came in 1609 from Hornacho in Estramadura and settled in the Qasba of the Oudaia. A second group, who came from the Cadiz area in 1610, settled nearby and were probably responsible for building the present Moorish medina of Rabat. On many of the doorways of the houses there are traces of Spanish Renaissance decoration; Rabat embroidery has patterns of the same origin; and there is a tradition, now almost lost, of making handsome wooden chests with spirally fluted legs which is very obviously of Spanish inspiration. Many Rabatis still have such Spanish names as Bargash (Vargas) or Rundi (of Ronda). Speaking Spanish as much as Arabic, this new community formed a distinct element; like the Tetuanis they devoted themselves to maritime trade and privateering. In the chaotic conditions of the time they formed for some fourteen years (1627–41) a semi-independent 'Republic of the Bu Regreg' under the nominal sovereignty of the Sultan. As privateers the people of this miniature republic, who were known as the Sallee Rovers, became quite formidable. These ships went far afield and in Daniel Defoe's story it was to Salé that Robinson Crusoe was brought as a captive. At first directed against Spain, their activities were then extended to other Christian shipping. In 1626 they captured three English ships in the Channel and others off Weymouth, Dartmouth, and Plymouth, and on the way to Newfoundland. Some of these prizes were sold to the Dutch. The cost of ransoming the crew of five ships taken off Glamorgan aroused angry protests. There was at this time in Morocco an English political agent, named John Harrison, who thought the circumstances could be turned to serve English interests and used against Spain. The Caids of Salé were in fact desperately anxious to secure supplies for their ships and to revenge themselves on the Spanish monarchy. The English government responded, and a treaty was drawn up by representatives of the Republic of the Bu Regreg; one of the signatories for the republic bore the half-Spanish, half-Arabic name of Shaib Vargas and the bearer of the letter to King James that of Ahmad Hussein Narvaes. The King did not ratify the treaty, since the Bu Regreg was not regarded as independent, but he approved their proposals. This was part of a general policy of the English crown towards the Barbary states, for in 1626 England made peace with Algiers and in 1628 Charles I issued an order that English ships were not to molest Algerian, Tunisian, Tetuani, or Sallee shipping. The idea that England should seek an accommodation with infidels aroused protests at home and abroad, amongst others from the Doge of Venice. English ship captains largely ignored the order and one of them promptly captured a Sallee ship and sold it to the Portuguese. When the Sallee captain produced a copy of King Charles's order, the English captain, it was reported, simply took it and 'wiped his tayle with it'. Such actions produced immediate reprisals against English merchants in Sallee and made John Harrison very angry. In despair the Moriscos in 1631 unsuccessfully begged Philip IV to let them return to Spain. The end soon came and in 1637 an English squadron was assisting the murábit al-Ayyashi to attack the town. In 1641 they lost the last trace of autonomy.

In the last century it became customary to write as if only the North African Muslims indulged in questionable forms of privateering and to refer to them as nothing more than pirates. In fact all the maritime powers engaged in privateering and they frequently behaved in a way which provoked the cry of 'piracy'. Many well-known Moroccans suffered from the activities of European privateers, among them Leo Africanus who has been mentioned above, and in the eighteenth century, the historian al-Zayyani. In the matter of violations of sea-law the Muslims were no worse offenders than others.

The little republic of the Bu Regreg came to an end in 1641 when the murábits of Dila, having defeated al-Ayyashi, got possession of the town. From them it was finally recovered by an Alawite Sultan who, in the time of Charles II, was assisted by an English force of 200 volunteers under a certain Captain Giffard.

The Alawite dynasty, which secured supreme power in Morocco in the middle of the seventeenth century, has ruled the country ever since, except for the recent period of the Franco-Spanish protectorate when the Sultans reigned but did not rule. The Alawites are a Sherifian family which had been settled since the fourteenth century near the modern Erfoud in Tafilalet; for this reason they are sometimes known as the Filali sherifs. In the confusion of the Saadian decadence Maulay Ali al-Sherif (whose tomb can be seen today in Rissani, the ancient Sijilmassa, near Erfoud) came to the fore as a leader; by 1667 his son, Maulay al-Rashid, after first establishing a Makhzen in Taza, succeeded in occupying Fez. In 1668 he destroyed the zawiya of Dila and by 1671 had occupied Marrakesh and brought the Sous under control.

It is however his brother and successor, Maulay Ismail, who reigned for the half century from 1672 to 1727, whose name is best known in Europe. In Morocco Maulay Ismail is regarded as a great and worthy ruler while he is referred to in many European works as a monster of cruelty. There is convincing evidence that he was in fact cruel, but the stress on this is largely because information about him in Europe was derived mainly from the European prisoners who were employed as slaves on his building projects at his capital Meknès, from the priests who attended them, and from the reports of the occasional Ambassador who visited Meknès and obtained his information from the same sources. The prisoners were treated much as Maulay Ismail treated his own Moroccan forced labourers (except that the Europeans were allowed to make wine and brandy for their own use); and the treatment of Moroccans by their rulers was harsh indeed. It was customary for ransomed or escaped prisoners to publish accounts of their experiences and it is clear that publishers expected them to paint Christian sufferings in vivid colours, and to flavour them with equally highly spiced accounts of their amorous adventures with the wives of their employers. Narratives by priests engaged in the work of redemption tended also to lay the colours on thick, in order to stimulate the feelings of the sympathizers who subscribed funds. It was not however an age of kindly treatment of prisoners anywhere. There were thousands of Muslim slaves in Malta in the same period and a Maltese historian has painted an appalling picture of their treatment when suspected of organizing a conspiracy – a mass punishment worse than anything ever attributed by European historians to the rulers of the Barbary states.[15] The French government used to purchase large numbers of these slaves to row in the galleys and at one time Louis XIV hesitated to redeem French captives for fear that he would have to surrender an equal number of Muslim galley-slaves.

John Evelyn, travelling in France in 1644, describes the conditions in the galleys where they were employed.[16]

The spectacle was to me new and strange, to see so many hundreds of miserably naked persons, their heads being shaved close, and having only high red bonnets, a pair of coarse canvas drawers, their whole backs and legs naked, doubly chained about their middle and legs, in couples, and made so fast to their seats, and all commanded in a trice by an imperious and cruel seaman.

They are ruled and chastised by strokes on their backs and soles of their feet, on the least disorder, and without the least humanity, yet are they cheerful and full of knavery.

We may suspect some exaggeration, too, in the number of wives, concubines, and children attributed to Maulay Ismail. Legend credited him with 1,056 children of one sex or the other; but the only trustworthy piece of evidence, that of a French prisoner long in the country, states that he had 'over sixty' children at the age of thirty-four or thirty-five; this suggests that he may have had two hundred by the end of his life. Equally fabulous numbers of women are said to have lived in his harem, and often to have been cruelly treated by him. These are not matters about which information is made public in Muslim countries, but we do get a glimpse of Maulay Ismail's private life through the eyes of another prisoner.[17] This was an Englishman by name Pellow, who was many years in Maulay Ismail's service, and accepted Islam, as he says, to escape ill-treatment. As a young man working in the palace garden he was noticed by the chief queen who begged him from the Sultan for her service. He then became head porter to this queen whose name he gives as Hellema Huzezza (presumably Halima Aziza), and was put in charge of the door of the apartments where she lived with thirty-seven other women whom he describes as concubines. The Sultan visited the Queen at stated times and was expected to give previous notice if he wished to come at other hours. On one occasion Pellow got much credit for refusing to open the door (though he recognized the Sultan's voice on the other side) when Maulay Ismail had failed to give previous warning. It is also interesting that according to Windus, who wrote an account of an English embassy to Maulay Ismail, the English ambassador, failing to get satisfaction from the Sultan on some matter, wrote a letter to one of the queens asking her intervention, which she gave. The embassy resulted in the termination of a state of war which had existed between Morocco and England for the previous seven years. This was of course a war of privateers.

There is no doubt that Maulay Ismail was a convinced Muslim who practised his religion in every detail and lived very plainly. He also possessed immense energy and vitality. He is described by a European who knew him as showing a great deal of wit and courage and as being active, indefatigable, and dexterous at all martial sports. After fifteen years of struggle he established his authority over the whole country with the exception of the High Atlas, and at the end of his reign it was said that food was cheap and plentiful and that it was 'possible for a Jew or a woman to walk from one end of the country to the other without as much as anyone questioning them'.[18] On the other hand, his subjects were said 'to work and pay taxes, every week, every month, and every year'. His army was mainly composed of black troops. These were slaves, some of whom were descended from those who arrived after Ahmad al-Mansur's conquest of the Sudan, while others were specially acquired, many during an expedition which Maulay Ismail made to Mauritania. Black boys and girls were carefully brought up, the boys being trained in military pursuits and the girls in domestic arts, and later married. The other section of the army was composed of Oudaia Arabs from the south. Security of communications was ensured by the building of many qasbas or forts at strategic points.

In external affairs Maulay Ismail was able to keep the Turks out of Morocco but failed to extend his own authority over Algeria. In 1681 he recovered Mamora (now Mahdiya), acquired by the Spanish in 1610; Larache in 1689; and Arzila in 1691. Tangier, which the English had received from the Portuguese as Catharine of Braganza's dowry in 1661, after resisting several heavy attacks, was abandoned to Maulay Ismail in 1684 and repopulated with people from the Rif. On the other hand Maulay Ismail failed to retake either Ceuta or Melilla. He maintained diplomatic relations with a number of countries and made an indirect approach to Louis XIV for the hand of his illegitimate daughter, the Princesse de Conti. He wrote long letters to both Louis and James II, urging them to adopt Islam or, in the latter's case, at least to revert to Protestantism which the Sultan regarded as less idolatrous than the Catholic faith. In spite of this, Maulay Ismail was personally well disposed to the Spanish Franciscan Friars who ministered to the prisoners. They had a convent and a parish church in Meknès, as well as two out of four chapels in

Meknès, the other two belonging to the Portuguese. They were able to found a new convent in Fez and to maintain chapels in Tetuan and Salé. In all these they were able 'to exercise the Catholic rites with the same correctness and liberty that they could in Spain'.[19]

Maulay Ismail had a passion for building. From the moment that security permitted, says a Moroccan historian, 'he devoted himself exclusively to building his palaces and planting his gardens'.[20] His constructions seem to have been more conspicuous for size than for beauty, though there still exist some very handsome gateways in Meknès. The Sultan supervised all stores himself and gave minute attention to detail. An English visitor described the palaces and offices as 'extremely magnificent, beautiful, and neat'.[21]

On his death Maulay Ismail left a library of 12,000 volumes which his son distributed to various mosque libraries.

The end of his fifty years reign was darkened by the behaviour of his sons and his death was followed by thirty years of anarchy. This was his own fault as well as that of his sons, for the privileged position which he had given the black troops and the Oudaia Arabs resulted in their now taking advantage of it to throne and dethrone Sultans, according to what they could hope to receive from them. The Middle Atlas tribesmen, always turbulent, took the opportunity to seek advantage for themselves and the resulting sufferings of the people were said to be such that they 'would whiten the hair of infants at the breast'.

A less disturbed period followed with the reigns of Sidi Muhammad III (1757–90) and of Maulay Sulaiman (1792–1822), though they were interrupted by the disastrous two years reign of the brilliant but half-mad al-Yazid. The rest of the nineteenth century was all but filled by the reigns of Maulay Abd al-Rahman (1822–59), of Sidi Muhammad IV (1859–73), and of Maulay al-Hassan I (1873–94).

All these five sovereigns were conscientious rulers and personally worthy. They endeavoured to reduce the subversive tendencies of the murábits and to keep the religious confraternities within the limits of what is reasonable. Muhammad III and his successor were attracted by the doctrine of the reforming Wahhabi movement in

Arabia. Nevertheless this period of 150 years is the least interesting in Moroccan history. The inspiration and the splendour of the Almoravid and Almohad periods are entirely lacking; nor is there the delicate decoration connected with Beni Merin building nor the Levantine brilliance of Ahmad al-Mansur nor the barbaric vitality of Maulay Ismail. Morocco did indeed develop trade relations with Europe, but the country retired into itself, spiritually and physically, and its energies were increasingly consumed in the negative task of preserving something of its medieval heritage in spite of the decadence which had overtaken it and its anachronistic character in modern times. No great new monuments were created; there were less chroniclers of Moroccan history than there had been earlier. The Sultans devoted the greater part of their time to military expeditions around the country (which were not always successful) in order to enforce respect and to collect taxes. Meanwhile the Makhzen was increasingly at the mercy of the vigorous modern states of Christian Europe. These were steadily substituting their influence for that of the Makhzen first in the ports, and round the Spanish presidios, and on the Algerian frontier, and then by one means or another in the interior.

The opening of the period was marked by the negotiation of numerous trade treaties – with Denmark in 1757, England in 1760, Sweden in 1763, Venice in 1765, France and Spain in 1767, the Two Sicilies and the USA in 1786. Morocco was one of the first states to recognize the independence of the USA, an action for which Muhammad III received a letter of thanks from George Washington. In 1774 a Moroccan demand for the return of Ceuta and Melilla provoked a Spanish declaration of war which was followed by a Moroccan attack on the two presidios. This failed, partly because the Spanish prevented a British squadron from delivering arms and ammunitions to the besiegers. Peace was restored in 1780. On the other hand, the tactlessness of the Governor of Gibraltar, during the great siege of the rock from 1779 to 1783, provoked the expulsion from Tangier and Tetuan of the British consul and 108 British subjects who had been supplying the garrison with useful information.

In 1765 Muhammad III founded the present city of Mogador (in Arabic al-Souira) which supplanted Agadir as the principal centre of foreign trade in the south during the succeeding 150 years. It was designed in part by a French and in part by a Muslim English architect; the latter is honoured by an Arabic inscription in which he is described as Ahmad al-Inglizi (Ahmad the English-man). Situated on what is almost an island, cool in summer and warm in winter, Mogador with its carefully planned streets and Andalusian appearance has in miniature something of the charm of Cadiz.

The port served the trade from the area of the Sous, of the Wadi Noun and the Wadi Dra, and from the Saharan oases, and from West Africa. This was sufficient to give it a leading place among Moroccan ports and to attract a number of English, French, and other merchants, as well as a Jewish community which in 1900 amounted to a third of the total population of about 30,000. Chiefly candles, cloth, and tea were imported from England; sugar and silk from France. The port began to lose importance when the French occupation of West Africa led to the interruption of the camel traffic from Timbuctu. This had previously consisted of caravans totalling 500 to 600 camels annually, loaded with ivory, ostrich feathers, and gold dust.

From 1792 to 1822, the period of the reign of Maulay Sulaiman, relations with the Muslim regencies to the east were good, while Europe was too much occupied with the Napoleonic wars to pay much attention to Morocco. Godoy however, the favourite of Charles IV of Spain, did try to persuade his master to invade Morocco, a plan which the kindly King rejected on moral grounds. This was fortunate for Spain as Sulaiman, though threatened by Napoleon with a French invasion, took Spain's side during the French occupation even when Joseph Bonaparte offered to return Ceuta and Melilla to Morocco if the Sultan would recognize him as Spanish King.

In 1806, at the request of the Ottoman Sultan then at war with Russia, Maulay Sulaiman consented to station his ships in the Straits hoping to stop any Russian vessels which might seek to pass through. None appeared, and nine years later (1817) he was forced by the ever-increasing technical superiority of the European fleets to agree to put an end to Moroccan privateering. In 1818 the country was sufficiently prosperous to supply wheat to France and a year or two later to Tunis. The last years of the reign were disastrous. Faced with a rising of Middle Atlas Berbers, Maulay Sulaiman was defeated in the Tadla region and actually taken prisoner. Berber respect for their Imam led his captors to treat him with great respect, even though they had been fighting his armies. The women crowded round to kiss the hem of his garments; the men begged his pardon, and escorted him back to his capital, Meknès. This did not prevent the tribes from attacking his forces between Fez and Meknès again in the following year.

The anarchy of these concluding years was redeemed by Maulay Sulaiman's nomination of a capable nephew as his successor in preference to his own less worthy sons. This was an unusual piece of altruism which made a deep impression on Moroccan opinion.

The reign of Maulay Abd al-Rahman (1822–59) saw the signing in 1856 of a treaty with England, whose government had by now assumed the position of protector of Moroccan independence while herself acquiring a privileged standing in the country. By this treaty England acquired certain trade privileges and the right of 'protecting' a number of Moroccan subjects. The treaty became a model for future agreements with other European states and thus led to the ultimate economic and political penetration of Morocco.

For a quarter of a century there had been signs of the impending collapse. In 1829, Maulay Abd al-Rahman, not realizing his weakness against a now greater strength, had authorized two ships to go privateering. They captured two Austrian sailing vessels off the coast, but the result was an Austrian bombardment of Larache and the destruction of the Moroccan ships. When the French in 1830 captured Algiers the people of Tlemsen asked for the Sultan's protection. After his experience of the previous year he gave this with some reluctance and withdrew it again when the lack of discipline of his troops caused the people of Tlemsen to complain. However, the Algerian leader, Abd al-Qadir did homage to the

Sultan and when his position later became desperate Muslim opinion gave the latter no option but to try the lot of war. The result was the ignominious defeat of a Moroccan army by General Bougeaud at Isly near Oujda in 1844, while French ships bombarded Tangier and Mogador. The Sultan now had to make peace on the humiliating condition that he would expel Abd al-Qadir or hand him over to the French if ever he sought refuge in Morocco. A previously non-existent frontier line was at the same time drawn from the coast towards the interior. In 1851 a misunderstanding, after the looting of two French ships wrecked near Salé, was followed by a French bombardment from the sea. By now it had become apparent that Morocco was at the mercy of any incident which gave a European power the excuse to intervene and that its chief means of defence was constituted by the disagreements of these powers among themselves.

Muhammad IV (1859–73) was faced, at the moment of his accession, by a Spanish declaration of war, following an incident on the frontier of the Ceuta enclave. On 5 February 1860 the Spanish army occupied Tetuan and were only prevented from advancing on Tangier by the intervention of the British government which objected to the possible installation of a European power on the Straits. Morocco had to pay an indemnity of £4,000,000 and to promise the cession of an area on the Atlantic coast corresponding to a fishing establishment which Spain had possessed there in the fifteenth century. After eighty years delay this led in 1934 to the Spanish occupation of Ifni.

After the war of 1860 the status of the European consulates, which were now established in Tangier, was raised to that of legations. In 1865 the diplomats secured the establishment of an internationally managed lighthouse at Cape Spartel and, in 1872, of a sanitary council. These privileges were the origin of the multi-national status of Tangier under the protectorate.

Maulay al-Hassan, who reigned from 1873 to 1894, was the last Sultan before the occupation who was able to preserve at least the appearance of independence to the Sherifian Empire – the 'Fortunate Empire' as it was styled in official documents. In the memory of his subjects Maulay al-Hassan 'left the reputation of a great sovereign;

his dignified exterior and his activity won him the respect of the Europeans who were in contact with him'. His success was due to his unceasing operations against dissident elements within the country and to his extreme caution in external affairs; whenever foreign powers found a pretext to intervene, he went out of his way to be conciliatory. Thus in 1876 he granted a French demand to install a representative at Oujda to deal with frontier incidents, though in fact the inability of the Makhzen to enforce any decisions taken made matters worse. In 1893, when Rifi tribesmen, out of control of the Makhzen, attacked the Spanish at Melilla and the Spanish government landed an army, he settled by the payment of an indemnity of £650,000. In 1880 he succeeded in calling a Conference at Madrid to discuss the abuses of the system of protection, but the only result was that the practice was regularized and extended to more countries.

Internally, Maulay al-Hassan did his best to retain control by incessant small expeditions and several major campaigns. In 1882 he took a force to the Sous, founding Tiznit as a local capital. In 1886 he took the army as far as Goulimin. The last great expedition was that of 1893 to Tafilalet. This was undertaken from Marrakesh; on the return journey the passage across the Atlas through the snow cost terrible losses. 'As the cold increased, soldiers, mules, horses, and camels died of exposure. Snow fell and covered the camp, and only by forced marches were the remnants of the great horde dragged out from the deathly grip of the rocks and snows of the Atlas mountains to the plains below. The Sultan had become an old man. Travel-stained and weary, he rode his great white horse with the mockery of green and gold trappings while above his head that was the picture of suffering waved the imperial umbrella of crimson velvet.'[22] Having arrived at Marrakesh he was forced to set out at once for the north to punish the Rifi tribes who had attacked the Spanish and involved the country in a heavy indemnity. On the way, he died at Tadla, and his sixteen-year-old son Abd al-Aziz was proclaimed Sultan.

The one striking innovation made by Maulay al-Hassan was the despatch to Spain of a certain number of Moroccan students to acquire western medical, engineering, and other sciences. With a Moroccan background it was difficult for these students to profit from European teaching and when they returned to Morocco the European ideas which they had acquired made it difficult for them to fit into the Moroccan environment again.

For eight years after Maulay Abd al-Aziz's accession government was carried on by Ba Ahmad in traditional fashion. Being himself of slave origin and a man of the south Ba Ahmad suspected that the Grand Vizir in Fez, with his brother the Minister of War, of the well-known Jamai family, might attempt to put a different member of the royal family on the throne. When after the young Sultan's arrival the two brothers presented themselves at the palace at Fez they were abruptly dismissed from office. Two days later they were arrested at their home, but not before the former Grand Vizir had attempted to resist. In the struggle his fine clothes were torn to shreds. With four ropes round his neck, each held by a soldier, he was dragged to prison among the derisive jeers of the people. The palaces which the two brothers built in Fez and Meknès have become a luxury hotel, well known to travellers, and a museum.

When the regent Ba Ahmad died in 1902, the young Sultan began to rule himself. Those Europeans who knew him agree that he was thoughtful, intelligent, considerate, and desirous of doing well. But he had neither the resolution nor the experience to deal with the coming crisis, nor had he the needful honest and capable assistants. The very year in which he took control was that in which the French decided to occupy the oases of Tuat in the central Sahara, an area regarded by the Makhzen as subject to Moroccan suzereignty. In view of the very loose character of this suzereignty the French did not see that their occupation need greatly disturb the Makhzen. The Moroccans however felt quite differently on the subject. A French observer, present in Morocco at the moment, wrote that it was: 'enough to strain the Moroccan conscience, to incite it to Holy War, to strain to breaking point the fragile link uniting the tribes to a Sultan who was unable . . . to fulfil the task for which the Sherifian dynasties had been raised to the throne. The perturbation was such that officials were unanimous in conceding the need for a new system and the urgency of reform.'[23]

Reforms had in fact been urged on the Makhzen for years past both by the British and other governments. Their suggestions included limitations on the arbitrary power of the Sultan, a modern system of taxation and modern methods of collecting it, the abolition of medieval punishments, more humane treatment of the tribes and of prisoners, and the payment of adequate salaries to officials instead of expecting them to make what they could out of their administration. Revolutionary as such ideas were to most Moroccans they accorded with the disposition of the young ruler.

Alas, the attempted reforms, inadequately prepared, misunderstood by the people, and without machinery to apply them merely discredited and weakened the Makhzen further. In future, decisions were to be taken by the Grand Vizir after consultation with the other ministers instead of by the Sultan. This freed the Sultan's afternoons for more agreeable pursuits, but did not tend to speedy or more disinterested decisions nor promote their prompt execution. The payment of salaries did not exclude corruption. The disturbance caused by the new system of taxation meant that for some time few taxes were collected at all. The young Sultan enjoyed the company of Europeans and a group of them became closely connected with the court. Some were honest advisers, others adventurers, others simply commercial agents. The afternoons were spent in bicycle polo, at which the Sultan became expert, but there were still no roads for wheeled traffic. Abd al-Aziz developed a passion for mechanical and scientific devices such as cameras, mechanical birds, and fireworks. He proposed to lay a few miles of Decauville railway from the palace; this involved trouble with the Ulama who held that it did not justify the expropriation of the lands of Muslims. As the resources of the treasury were squandered in transporting billiard tables or circuses from the ports to Fez, the Makhzen became indebted, and the surest source of income, the customs, was soon pledged to foreigners as security for loans. Meanwhile European encroachments increased on all sides and the Moroccan people began to react in the traditional manner. In the towns much discontent was caused by the great rise in the cost of living resulting from the increased trade with Europe and the presence of Europeans in the coastal areas. The tribes became restless and sporadic attacks were made on foreigners. Soon a pretender, known as Bu Hamara the Rogui, set up a rival Makhzen in Taza, and threatened Fez.

Meanwhile the British government which had been supporting the independence of the Muslim governments in North Africa and the Middle East for over a century, preferring them to possible European rivals, decided that they were becoming too decrepit to maintain. This led to Britain acquiescing in French intervention in Tunis (in return for French acquiescence in the British occupation of Cyprus) and then to British intervention in Egypt. Now it was Morocco's turn. In April 1904, in return for a free hand in Egypt, the British government undertook to leave France free to act in Morocco, provided always that no fortifications were erected on the Straits. In October of the same year the French and Spanish govern/ ments agreed on respective 'spheres of influence' in Morocco. A French agreement with Italy secured Italian acquiescence in French plans in return for French acquiescence in Italian plans in Libya. In 1905 the spectacular visit of the Kaiser to Tangier and his declaration in favour of the Sultan's independence raised the Makhzen's hopes that here was a new defender; in reality there was only a new claimant to share in the spoils. With German aid the Sultan now secured the calling of the Conference of Algeciras at which France, Spain, the United Kingdom, Russia, Austria/ Hungary, Portugal, Italy, Germany, Sweden, the Netherlands, and Belgium were represented. Though a failure from the Moroccan as well as from the German point of view, the Act of Algeciras had some favourable as well as some unfavourable influence on the future of Moroccan independence. It established a Franco/Spanish police force for the Moroccan coastal towns which prepared the way for Franco/Spanish intervention on a larger scale. But it also gave all the countries present a say in Moroccan affairs, internationalizing the problem, and limiting the power of individual action of any country that might intervene.

In the next year, 1907, attacks on European workmen in Casa/ blanca led to the French occupation of the town and the surrounding country. More or less simultaneously French troops from Algeria occupied Oujda. This provoked another traditional reaction. The

Sultan's brother Maulay Abd al-Hafidh, governor of Marrakesh, declared that his brother, the Sultan, was squandering the country's resources and delivering it to the infidel. He therefore raised the standard of revolt and declared himself ruler. In due course the two brothers marched with their respective forces towards one another's capitals. When they met, Abd al-Aziz's force melted away and he himself took refuge with the French. Abd al-Hafidh, after his army had made a completely unsuccessful attack on the French, occupied Fez where he was recognized as Sultan. His only subsequent success was the capture of the pretender from Taza. The latter was brought to Fez in an iron cage, specially constructed by a local Italian armourer, and was exhibited to the populace before being executed. This, and the barbarous punishments inflicted on the captives, destroyed any credit that Maulay Abd al-Hafidh might otherwise have acquired from the success. In 1909 Rifi tribesmen attacked Spaniards working in the iron-mines, under a concession from the pretender Bu Hamara. Thereupon the Spanish government landed a force of 90,000 men and forcibly enlarged the boundaries of Melilla; the city was thus enabled to expand outside the narrow limits of the rock to which it had hitherto been confined. In 1910 a new pretender appeared in Meknès. More or less besieged in Fez, Maulay Abd al-Hafidh invoked French help and a French force relieved the city. The Spanish government thereupon ensured French respect for the 1904 agreement by themselves occupying Larache and Alcazar-quivir. In July 1911 one last international scurry occurred, when a German gunboat appeared off Agadir. Important in European politics this event had little effect on the course of events in Morocco; the Germans were simply bought out by the French with a piece of colonial territory in the Congo.

Seeing no hope of succour on the horizon in any direction, Maulay Abd al-Hafidh in the spring of 1912 signed the Treaty of Fez by which Morocco became a French protectorate, except that vaguely defined rights were guaranteed to the Spanish government in the northern area, adjoining the Mediterranean.

A thousand years of history had come to an end. The old Morocco had passed away; the new Morocco was not yet born.

46 One of the great Alawite rulers Maulay Ismail established diplomatic relations with other principal European powers. In this seventeenth-century engraving, the French ambassador is received at the palace of Maulay Ismail in Meknès.

47 Ruins of the vast store-houses at the palace of Maulay Ismail in Meknès.

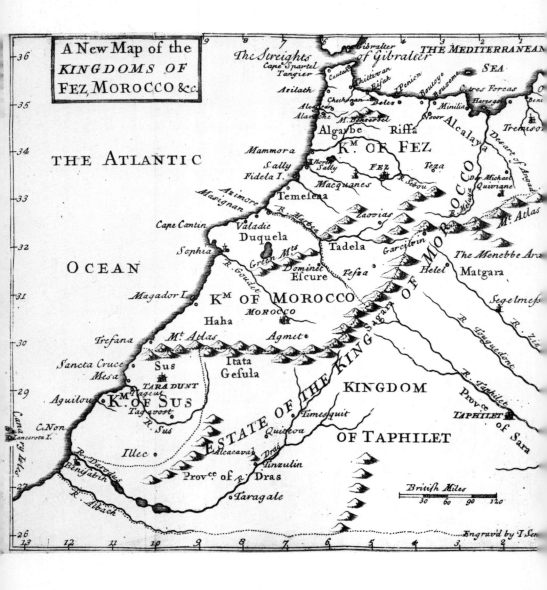

48 In the sixteenth and seventeenth centuries Morocco was divided into separate
kingdoms which were reunited by the Alawite rulers.

49 In the eighteenth and nineteenth
centuries Fez continued to be the centre
of intellectual, commercial and cultural
life. This is a contemporary engraving of
an opulent Jewish house.

50 An eighteenth-century engraving
illustrating various aspects of life and
custom in Fez.

51 Maulay Ismail also wrote letters to Louis XIV of France and James II of England urging them to adopt Islam. This is one to Louis XIV dated 1693.

52 The Moroccan admiral Abdala ben Aischa was also Moroccan ambassador in France in the seventeenth century as shown in this contemporary engraving.

LAMBASSADEVR de Maroc disne auec Sa suitte et Seruy par quatre Esclaues Turc a paris 1699

Abdala Ben Aischa Amiral et Surintandant Generalde
la marine de lempire de Maroc Ambassadeur de Maroc en France en 1699
2 Mahameth Touriris Capitaine de Vaisseaux L'ieutenant de l'Ambassade
3 Achmeth Soussin Docteur de la Loy Secretaire de l'Ambassade
4 Esclaues Maures seruent lambassadeur au dîne sur les Sopha 5 Esclaues luy
porte le Sobet pour boire — 6 Esclaues luy alume sapipe apres le repas — seuend chez Leroux

53 In 1765 the Alawite Sultan Muhammad III founded the city of Al-Souira (Mogador) which became the centre for foreign trade in the South.

54 By the beginning of the nineteenth century Morocco was the prey of contending European powers and particularly the French. This nineteenth-century engraving illustrates the Moroccan defeat by the French at Isly in 1844.

55 In 1912 most of Morocco became a French protectorate and the first Resident General was Louis Hubert Gonsalve Lyautey.

56 When Tafilalet was occupied by the French, General Lyautey was met by the governor.

57 Tangier became a separate zone, with an international régime on account of its previous status as the seat of European legations. The native quarter or Quasba at Tangier.

58 Melilla has been a Spanish possession since 1496. Frontier adjustments were made two years after the Spanish-Moroccan war in 1860 as shown in this nineteenth-century engraving.

Entrevue de Muley-el-Abbas avec le gouverneur de Melilla (Maroc). (Délimitation des frontières espagnoles et marocaines). — (Croquis de M. Juan Alvarez.)

Délimitation des frontières de Melilla (Maroc).
ENTREVUE DU GOUVERNEUR AVEC MULEY-EL-ABBAS.

La grave question de Melilla est entrée dans sa période décroissante; les empiétements continuels des Riffeins que les Espagnols étaient décidés à réprimer, dussent-ils leur coûter une seconde guerre aussi sanglante que la première, ont été l'objet de la part de l'empereur du Maroc de terribles répressions et, cette fois encore (car on ne saurait espérer que cette entente soit définitive), les Riffeins chassés par leurs propres maîtres rentreront dans leurs limites, s'y maintiendront et une nouvelle délimitation sera établie; on décidera la question d'établissement de redoutes destinées à défendre de toute nouvelle atta-

cate ont déterminé entre le général gouverneur de Melilla et le frère de l'empereur du Maroc, spécialement délégué à cet effet, une entrevue dont un officier espagnol veut bien nous envoyer un croquis.

La génération actuelle a vu s'asseoir autour des tapis verts bien des diplomates chargés de débattre les intérêts de leurs nations.

Les mêmes formules et les mêmes protocoles s'y reproduisent avec le même cérémonial, les guerres européennes où se résolvent des intérêts bien autrement puissants n'offrent pas d'aussi pittoresques spectacles; on aimera peut-être à assister par le dessin à ces solennités qui ont pour théâtre un splendide horizon et pour spectateurs deux armées séparées par les plus cruelles divisions, mais plus éloignées encore par leurs croyances, leurs mœurs, leurs instincts, leurs habitudes.

59 A profound impression was made upon the French painter Eugène Delacroix who visited Morocco in 1832. This is one of three versions of a painting of the Sultan Maulay Abd al-Rahman.

7   The Scene changes

SOMBRE MOROCCO, long may you remain immured, impenetrable to novelty! Turn your back on Europe; abide motionless in time past! Long may your sleep continue; your ancient dream persist, that there may be still one last land where men pray.

Allah preserve for the Sultan his lands of dissidence and his solitudes carpeted with flowers, his wildernesses of asphodels and irises, that he have space to display the agility of his horsemen and his horses; to fight as the champions of old fought and to harvest the heads of rebels. Allah preserve their mystical dreams to the Arab people, their disdainful immobility, and their dusty rags! May he preserve their sad tremulous voice to the pipes of the nomads; to the ancient mosques their inviolate mystery – and to the ruined walls their shroud of white chalk.[24]

With these words, Pierre Loti closed his account of a visit to Fez in 1889. Romantic as his vision was, he accurately portrayed an aspect of Morocco which struck all those Europeans who visited it at that period.

The four centuries of Moroccan greatness from the eleventh to the fifteenth century had been followed by a prolonged twilight. There was a moment at the end of the sixteenth century when it seemed as if Morocco might be about to step into the modern world, in company with the other states of the west. This did not happen; Morocco was fated to be afflicted with more than her fair share of the decadence which affected the whole of the Arab world, and to enter the twentieth century almost untouched by the modern life which was already stirring in the east. Not only did the system of government and the way of life of the people remain medieval but it fell far below its own former standards. Moroccan builders could still erect a building of beauty; the work of the craftsmen could still be exquisite; a tradition of good breeding and good manners was preserved. But the great monuments of the past were neglected, and were not replaced by new, as in the west, nor by any fresh form of life. Arab learning did not entirely disappear. Morocco produced one historian of distinction in the nineteenth century, but there was no printing press and no newspaper. A handful of classical works were lithographed in Fez. The country's military forces could no longer repel a foreign invader; fleets that had once been able to hold their own against Spain had simply ceased to exist. The Makhzen possessed one gunboat.

The decadence which overtook the whole Muslim world was accentuated in Morocco by its geographical position. Renovating forces could not enter from the west because of the ocean, nor from the south because of the desert and of the lack of civilization beyond it. National resistance first to the Turks and then to the French sealed the already difficult frontier on the east; religious and national sentiment barred the door to the north.

At the beginning of the twentieth century the Makhzen consisted first and foremost of the Sultan. In executive matters his authority was absolute. In the legislative field his actions were theoretically limited by the *sharia* or religious law. Not the Sultan but the *Ulama* (religious leaders) were the authorized interpreters of this; a ruler might and often did overrule their interpretation or bring such pressure to bear on them as to cause them to say what they did not think. Nevertheless a Sultan always did so at his risk. We have seen how Yusuf ibn Tashfin consulted the Ulama before deposing the Spanish princes. In the Saadian period Sultans often found it necessary to carry on a lengthy correspondence with the murábits in the effort to justify their actions. Maulay al-Hassan regularly explained and defended his policy in lengthy letters addressed to his subjects. When he wished to introduce legislation on the subject of narcotics he consulted the Ulama for guidance in overcoming certain difficulties and in safeguarding his own responsibility. Unfortunately the

Ulama shared in the general decadence and became an almost completely obscurantist influence.

In carrying out his will the Sultan had the services of several secretaries of state – a Chief Minister; a Minister of the Sea (foreign affairs), who resided in Tangier; a Minister of Finance, a Minister of War, and a Minister of Complaints (justice). Their offices (*beniqa*) in the palace consisted of little more than the means of writing, a chest for documents, and at the most some thirty secretaries. Under Maulay al-Hassan the ministers had to keep strict hours, morning and evening, and to be available for consultation by the Sultan when required. They received virtually no salary and if disgraced their property was seized. Municipal affairs were managed by a governor who also dealt with crime. *Qadis* (religious judges) dealt with personal affairs under the *sharia*. The duties of doorkeepers and so forth were carried out by officials known as *mokhaznis* or government men. Women were always veiled and only left home to go to the baths or to weddings, or to visit the cemeteries or for similar purposes. There was virtually no wheeled traffic. Ministers rode to their offices on mules and like everyone else wore traditional costume. Correspondence was sent by runner; latterly several foreign governments acquired the right to maintain post offices in the coastal towns. The provinces were governed by Caids whose administration was modelled on that of the Sultan. Only in part of the country were these governors officials of the central government and executants of its orders; in the rest they were local leaders who might or might not seek confirmation of their position from the Sultan. The nature of the situation in the latter areas was well described by the English surgeon Lemprières who treated the royal family in Tarudant in 1789. 'They acknowledge the emperor to be their sovereign', he wrote, 'and head of their church, and occasionally they pay him tribute as such; but they pay no attention whatever to his particular orders and over their internal government he has not the slightest control.' Such areas were known as *blad-al-siba*, generally translated as 'areas of dissidence' and so regarded by the Makhzen; in origin the word *siba* seems to mean the condition of potentially domestic animals which pasture uncontrolled. The court, like that of our Plantagenets, was constantly on the move and there were four recognized capitals, Fez, Meknès, Marrakesh, and Rabat. Certain cities were considered *hadriya* or cities of urban refinement; these were those in which a large population of Spanish Muslims had settled. There was a small regular army which after the Spanish-Moroccan war of 1860 acquired a few European instructors, such as the Scot, Caid Sir Harry Maclean. The bulk of this army consisted of contingents from tribes which were in return excused certain taxation; they had little discipline and were liable to return home to collect the harvest or whenever they liked.

The supervision of markets was entrusted to an official known as the *Muhtasib* who worked through the guilds of craftsmen, traders, and workers. In this persistence of the system of guilds and corporations we see a more pleasing aspect of medieval tradition. These institutions gave their members the self-respect of people who feel that they have a recognized place in society and a certain corporate spirit.

Like their Sultan the Moroccan people were intensely religious in the sense of scrupulously observing such duties as the ritual prayers and the keeping of the Ramadan fast. Moroccan society moved within a framework fixed by long-established religious ideas and ways of thought. There had thus been established a code of action and behaviour (*caida*) which could not be violated without incurring general reprobation. In observing this a feeling of self-respect was aroused amongst Moroccans which led them to avoid any action likely to be regarded as showing a lacking sense of shame (*hashuma*).

Though no type of organization could seem simpler than the Makhzen, its manipulation, as in other medieval states, was highly complicated. A French observer wrote at the time,

There was a veritable collection of small autonomous states, with regard to which the Makhzen had to proceed with diplomatic methods appropriate to each. Success involved winning the co-operation of the most influential by granting them certain privileges. In the military field the co-operation of the Makhzen tribes had to be secured; in the administrative, that of the Caids; in the religious, that of the sherifs (*shurfa*) and of the zawiyas. At the same time caution had to be used to keep these privileged associates under such control that they could not get the Makhzen itself at their mercy.[25]

The method was exemplified in the military expeditions which the Makhzen conducted. The primary purpose was to make a display of force in order to begin negotiations in a favourable position. As the army lived off the villagers in the meanwhile the method too often recalled that of 'making a solitude and calling it peace'. There was nevertheless in Morocco a very real order of a kind. In the expedition to Tafilalet some thousands of persons were moved across the Atlas, and even after allowance had been made for the disaster of the return journey this was a substantial achievement. 'The setting in motion and travel of this nomad power', said the same French observer, 'was carried out with a real order behind an apparent anarchy which is the characteristic of every manifestation of the Moroccan state.'[25]

One aspect of Moroccan medievalism which did the country much harm in the eyes of twentieth-century Europeans was the public employment of the barbarous methods of punishment of the Middle Ages, such as the display of the heads of defeated rebels on the city gates. Here is a description dated February 1903 from Fez, describing the scene in the capital after a defeat had been inflicted on the forces of the pretender:

Next morning there arrived the forty heads which formed the spoil of the victory packed in double baskets of esparto grass, hanging across the baggage animals. As soon as they had been unpacked, the forty heads were salted according to custom by Jews requisitioned for this purpose. . . . In the course of the afternoon they were attached to the battlements of Bab Mahruq, the usual place for such displays. Towards evening half a dozen Jews, dressed in black, climbed above the gate and removed the existing heads which witnessed, by their mere state of decomposition, the long lack of success of the Makhzen. Then, slowly and methodically, they replaced them by new heads which they fixed in the interstices of the stones. Underneath, a numerous crowd had assembled and was squatting on the ground, watching with placid curiosity and commenting periodically on the quality of the suspended heads. A young head would call forth approving murmurs from the public who considered it a worthwhile prize, while an old man's head provoked mocking smiles.[25]

In judging these proceedings it is well to recall that in some respects the practice was very similar, a couple of centuries earlier, in

England. In his Life, published in 1714, the well-known Quaker, Thomas Ellwood describes a scene which he witnessed in Newgate Prison. He mentions how the dead bodies of some executed and quartered criminals remained in the next room to his for some days, while the relations sought permission to remove and bury them. Leave for the 'quarters' to be buried was finally given, but not for the heads which were ordered to be set up in the city.

I saw the heads when they were brought up to be boiled. The hangman fetched them in a dirty dust basket, out of some by-place; and setting them down among the felons he and they made sport with them. They took them by the hair, flouting, jeering, and laughing at them; and then giving them some ill names, boxed them on the ears and cheeks. Which done the hangman put them into his kettle and parboiled them with Bay, Salt and Cummin seed: that to keep them from putrefaction, and this to keep the fowls from seizing them. The whole sight (as well that of the bloody quarters first, as the heads afterwards) was both frightful and loathsome.[26]

Of course the decadence into which Morocco had fallen had nothing to do with the merits of individuals. Some of the severest criticism of Moroccan life around 1800 was voiced by the English surgeon Lemprières who was called in 1789 to attend the Sherifian family in Tarudant. But, he adds, 'there are certainly among the Moors many people whose private virtues would do honour to any nation'. He also considered that the humanity which the Moors showed in their treatment of domestic slaves was something which put Europeans of that period to shame. Walter Harris, *The Times* correspondent in Morocco in the first decades of the twentieth century and a severe critic of Moroccan shortcomings, has this to say of two of his companions on the dangerous journey which he made with them in disguise to Tafilalet, his life being in their hands. He describes one of them as:

a long tall delicate thin man of twenty-four, a man of absolute fearlessness in danger, and of equal gentleness and sweetness of manner in time of peace. He never complained of cold or hunger, though we suffered much from both, but bore all the hardships of the journey, and they were many indeed, not only with every fortitude, but also without ever losing an opportunity to attempt to add to my comfort.

Of a returning *Hajj* or pilgrim, who was accompanying him, he says:

a strange quiet man, always ready to help us load our animals or pitch our little tent, but seldom speaking; never missing the hour of prayer, and often himself bearing part of the load of his little donkey, on which he was carrying to his native village a few bars of rough iron to be forged into ploughshares. . . . We often talked together as I trudged beside him, and he seemed to be a man of no little power of reasoning and thought. Often in discussing theological matters, and he would talk of nothing else, it became apparent that a battle was waging in his heart, a battle of common-sense against prejudice and fanaticism.[27]

The country in 1900 was still medieval in the contrast between the scene in the packed streets of the walled towns, whose gates were closed at night, and the sheer countryside outside. In Fez, the streets were narrow, with no windows opening on to them, and no indication that after passing through a winding entrance, one might step into a sunlit courtyard, scented with orange blossom, diversified by a fountain splashing into a basin, set above a blue and white tiled pavement. Travellers from Europe complained of the heaps of rubbish in the streets, but this did not necessarily mean that the interior was without a refinement any more than a similar heap did in the streets of Stratford outside our own Shakespeare's house. Here is a Eugène Aubin's account, written in 1903.

Our stay in Fez was enough to enable us to enter Moorish society. I cannot express the pleasure which I experienced in a form of living which, however degenerate, was once so glorious and still remains so impervious to European influences and so distinct from our own. I have spent most agreeable hours in very fine houses, where I have been invited to an excellent dinner accompanied by the strangest music. I have shared in the refined life of the Fasis. I have received information about details of dress from men reserved and cultured, whose flowing garments enhance their dignity, who enjoy the pleasures of good music and good cheer without ostentation, who are attentive and polite, leave their slippers at the door to avoid soiling the carpet with the mud of the street, come in softly, exchange some polite formula with their host or kiss him on the shoulder, and, if they have something to say, enter into conversation in a low tone to avoid disturbing the general quiet. . . . The patio is lighted by several lanterns, placed on the ground, while tapers in a room at the other end produce an effect of indefinite depth in the obscurity of the night. From a neighbouring room comes the sound of music softened by the distance, as it mingles with the splash of the water that falls from the fountain or bubbles within the basin in the centre of the court.[28]

Such houses, as the one here described have existed in Fez for centuries and still do, though the habit is spreading today of opening windows to the exterior and the lanterns and tapers are being re-placed by electric light. A French captive of Maulay Ismail thus described such a house more than 250 year ago.

The Houses . . . are square and terras'd at the Top; the Walls next to the Streets, or other Neighbours, have no windows. They have generally four Rooms below, eight or twelve foot wide, and twenty-five or thirty in length, some more, some less. The doors of these rooms are directly in the middle, that the light which comes in at them may equally reach both ends of the Chamber. The Courts are in the middle, in which there are commonly wells or if they be houses of great Men, which are always very spacious, there are Marble Basons, with Spouts of Water and some Fish ponds, about which they have Orange and Lemon Trees with the Fruit hanging on them all the year about. If the Houses be two Stories high, they have Galleries supported by Pillars of Marble, Freestone or Brick, with Turn'd wooden Bannisters on them, painted of several Colours. The Joists and Girders are painted after the same manner, there being an Ornament all round the Room, three Spans broad under them, of Plaister Fretwork in Flowers, after the Mosaick manner. Under that is another Circle, about a Man's height, of curious Checquer Work painted of several Colours, and representing all sorts of Flowers. They have Folding Doors which are always open, there being colour'd Silk Curtains before them. At both ends of the Rooms there are Estradoes, that is, a part raised about two spans above the Floor, made of Fir painted. On these Estradoes the great Men have their Beds, which consist of a Mat of painted Rushes, and several Carpets like those of Turkey. On them they lay Quilts not above two Inches thick, covered on the one side with Silk, cut in slips of several Colours, and on the other with Cotton Cloth, and Pillows stuff'd with Wooll. By them they have Haiques of Holland, or French linnen, which are Pieces of that Linnen, in which, after stripping to their Shirts, they wrap themselves up to sleep, and, for the more Conveniency, they make their Wives Beds at the other end of the Room, whither they go to them when they have a mind. . . .[29]

Speaking of the ladies themselves, the same writer continues:

The Moorish and Arabian women, especially those that live in Towns, are very Beautiful, Fair and Genteel in their Habit. The fattest are most admired and for this reason therefore they never wear anything that may confine their bodies but give themselves full liberty to spread. . . . Going abroad they cover them-selves with very fine large white veils, call'd Haiques, being bound about the middle of the face, that they may not be seen, leaving only their Eyes bare, to see the Way. They never speak to any Man in the Street, not even to their own Husbands, who cannot know tho' they meet them, because they are all clothed alike. They keep themselves very clean and often wash in their Baths. . . .

In a house such as that described above it is certain that one course at least would have been the traditional Moroccan *cuscus*, still the national dish today as it was when our Frenchman described its making:

They take a great Wooden Bowl, or Earthen Pan, before them, with a Por-ringer full of Flower (flour); and another of fair Water; a Sieve, and a Spoon. Then they put two or three Handfulls of the Flower into the Bowl, and pour three or four Spoonfuls of Water on it, which they work well with their Fingers, every now and then sprinkling it with Water, till it all runs into little Lumps like small Pease, and this they call Couscousou. As it rolls up they take it out of the Bowl and put it into the Sieve to separate the Flower that may remain loose; and there are some Women so expert at making it, that it is no bigger than Hail shot, which is the best. In the meanwhile they boil a great deal of good Meat, as Pullets, Beef, and Mutton, in a Pot that is not above a Span open at the Mouth, and so narrow at the bottom that it may sink two Inches within the Mouth of the other, the bottom whereof is full of holes like a Cullender. Into this last Pot they put the Couscousou over the other Pot the Meat boyls in, when it is almost Ready, leaving it so about three quarters of an Hour, close cover'd with a Napkin, and a wet Cloth with a little Flower, being wrapped about the Mouth of the other Pot, that no Steam may come out that way, but all ascend to pierce the Coucousou. When ready they turn it out into a Dish, and stir it about, that it may not cling together, but lie loose in Grains: Then they Butter it, and lastly pour on the Broth and all the Meat.[29]

If cuscus is the dish of rich and poor alike, varying only in its accessories, there are other dishes which are the pride of the Moroccan household, *tajin* (stew) of many varieties, chickens roasted with almonds and with lemons or with prunes, or meat with quinces, and above all *bastilla* – a dish with a Spanish name which is nevertheless unknown in Spain. The latter consists externally of pastry in very thin layers, lightly sprinkled with sugar. Within it has pigeon and eggs and cinnamon and almonds and many other ingredients. Its preparation takes not less than a whole day and when it is at its best it is incomparable.

Today, though not in Maulay Ismail's time, the meal always ends with the drinking of sweet tea, infused with mint, which is the national drink of Morocco. Perhaps, after China, no country has made such a ritual out of the preparation of tea as Morocco. Introduced by English merchants, the taste for tea became so widespread that the French, already casting a covetous eye on Morocco, accused the English of attempting to colonize the country through the sale of tea. Its cult is as firmly implanted among the Berbers of the countryside as it is among the rich merchants of Fez. In some Berber verses collected by a Spaniard in Ifni[30] we find the Englishman blamed for spreading a habit which consumes the wealth of those who can ill spare it. 'The Englishman was far too clever,' one verse says, 'when he sent us tea to plague us.' 'Expensive it is' says another, 'and money is hard to come by. I sold the cow, I sold the animals. We must have cups too; without cups we can do nothing; cups are the attendants of the teapot. . . . He who wants tea must build a little house to receive his friends; he who wants tea must spend much money.' There is a natural poetry about Berber life, which is reflected in their folk poetry:

> The story of tea I tell you.
> The rules of tea, thus they begin: –
> A house, where there are trees and plants
> And abundance of pure water.
> Let there be birds there which sing in their cages;
> A tray with fair China cups,
> And let it be youth, richly clad, that makes the tea.

In Fez as late as 1930 you might in the early afternoon see two or three well-to-do merchants passing out through the gates of the city to a spot beneath the olive trees where there was a wide view over city and plain. They would be accompanied by servants carrying a carpet, a teapot and cups, and a kettle, and canaries in a cage to sing to them, as they sipped their tea and enjoyed the view.

In trying to picture pre-occupation Morocco, I have made frequent use of the writings of a Frenchman, Eugène Aubin, who visited the country in 1903. His final words are particularly apt. He wrote:

Having finished this book about my Moroccan journey, I want to say what pleasure it gave me. The long rides across a countryside that was perpetually in flower; the encampment formed at sunset when the day's journey ended; the study of this Muslim civilization, immobilized in the remote Middle Ages; the very uncertainty as to the outcome of the present upheaval – nothing could be better adapted to reveal the incomparable charm of Morocco to those who find the supreme joy of life in movement and in effort.

However fascinating the old Morocco might seem to romantically minded travellers, it was apparent to diplomats from the end of the nineteenth century that it could not remain inviolate much longer.

Signs of a coming revolution in Morocco had indeed been visible as early as the time when Maulay al-Hassan sent Moroccan students to study in Spain and other foreign countries. Maulay Abd al-Aziz made the few foreigners at his court at Fez wear European clothes instead of adopting Moroccan dress, as had hitherto been the rule, in order as he said to get the people of Fez accustomed to the idea of modern clothes and to having foreigners in their midst. It was simply lack of will power, experience, and trained helpers, not of intention, which prevented him from modernizing his administration. In Maulay Abd al-Hafidh's day a few voices were even raised in favour of a constitution and a modern code of laws.

None of these portents was given any importance by the great powers in whose hands Morocco's immediate future lay. In the heyday of European domination it became a dogma that the east was unchanging. As this was a convenient justification for imperial rule, no incongruity was seen in reckoning Morocco among the 'eastern' countries, though geographically it was as western as any part of Europe. Virtually nobody foresaw that the four hundred year old process of European political expansion was about to undergo a sudden and almost total eclipse.

In these circumstances it was natural that the Treaty of Fez, signed in 1912, should be a good example of the type of protectorate treaty which had been evolved during the period of European expansion. A business-like and arid little document, it stated that the French government (always mentioned first) and the Sultan were anxious to inaugurate a regular régime in Morocco based upon internal order and security. For this purpose such 'administrative, judicial, educational, economic, financial, and military' reforms would be introduced as the French government might see fit. The régime to be established would safeguard the religious status, respect, and traditional prestige of the Sultan and the exercise of the Muslim religion. The French government moreover pledged itself to lend constant support to His Sherifian Majesty and to his heir and successors against any dangers which might threaten his person or throne or imperil the tranquillity of his domains. The French government would 'come to an understanding' with the Spanish government concerning the 'interests arising from the latter's geographical position and territorial possessions on the Moroccan coast'. Tangier would retain its 'distinctive characteristics' and these would 'determine its municipal organization'.

The former of the two final provisions was met by the establishment of a Spanish zone in the north. In this zone the Sultan made a standing delegation of all his powers to a *Khalifa* or Viceroy towards whom a Spanish High Commissioner stood in the same relationship as the French Resident General did to the Sultan. As for Tangier its 'special characteristics' (which meant the privileged position which the foreign diplomatic corps had acquired and the 'special sanitary organization' which they had established) were greatly increased by a Statute which was issued in 1923 after much international wrangling. Even then it was not recognized by the USA or, till later, by the Italian government. It empowered the signatories of the Act of Algeciras (less Russia, Germany, and Austria-Hungary, who had been victims of World War I), to control the administration of Tangier and the surrounding country through their diplomatic agents. The Sultan was represented by a *Mendub* or Delegate, appointed in practice by the French Resident General who was himself officially the Sultan's Foreign Minister as well as the representative of France. Thus while the integrity of the empire as stipulated by the Act of Algeciras was nominally preserved, in fact the country was divided into three distinct protectorates, one French, one Spanish, and one multi-national. The existence of the latter as an enclave in the Spanish zone was a great inconvenience to the Spanish authorities and a constant cause of grievance to them.

The provisions of the Treaty were designed to ensure the maximum French control compatible with French obligations under the Act of Algeciras and with her undertakings to individual European powers and bore the marks of exclusive French drafting. The Sultan was treated as sole spokesman for the Moroccan people, while the *Ulama* or religious leaders, whose opinion he should have taken on a matter of such fundamental importance as handing the administration over to a non-Muslim power, were entirely ignored. The Makhzen failed, if it ever attempted, to get a time limit inserted or to define conditions in which the protectorate might be terminated, though the idea must have been in Maulay Abd al-Hafidh's mind. At an earlier stage he had consulted his Foreign Minister about the withdrawal of French troops on the restoration of order. 'The French must have the matter in mind,' replied the Minister. 'The occupation is provisional.' 'H'm,' replied the Sultan, who was an Arabic scholar and a writer of devotional verse but also at times displayed a disconcerting cynicism, 'when God created the world, that was provisional too.'

When the French did take over the government of Morocco, they were able to draw on long experience in Muslim lands. As first Resident General, they appointed a great soldier and administrator with long previous experience in Algeria and elsewhere. General (later Marshal) Louis Hubert Gonsalve Lyautey was a man of exceptional independence of judgment; he possessed also an artistic sensibility which made him highly appreciative of the charm and traditions of Morocco and its people. It is largely to him that we owe the preservation of Morocco's monuments and the care taken in building new cities to make them harmonize as far as possible with the existing lay-out and with the Moroccan landscape. Coming at a moment when French technical skill was immeasurably ahead of that of Moroccans, he laid the foundations of an organization which achieved spectacular results with the minimum possible shock to national traditions and indigenous institutions. This achievement has been described in a great many books and has its place in French history. It was the more remarkable in that France for nine of the forty-four years of the protectorate was involved in the two World Wars. Here a very brief outline must suffice as background to an examination of the reactions of the Moroccan people in these entirely new circumstances.

In the first two years after the signing of the Treaty of Fez the foundations of the protectorate were well laid. On the outbreak of World War I in 1914, it was possible for France not only to retain control of all the area formerly administered by the Makhzen and now in French occupation and to repel attacks from the still unoccupied dissident areas, but also to make a considerable number of the garrisoning troops available for service at the French front. Though both during this period, and until 1934, there was much fighting in outlying areas, the whole country was by degrees brought under control and a highly efficient administration was created. By the end of the protectorate the country was equipped with first-rate ports, excellent roads, and an adequate railway system. The finances of the state were brought into order. The subsoil was exploited and Morocco became one of the leading exporters of mineral phosphates. A substantial industry was created in and around Casablanca; while the township of 20,000 inhabitants itself became a great modern city with a population of almost a million. The basis of a first-class educational system was laid. A modern legal system was introduced for cases in which foreign residents or foreigners and Moroccans were jointly involved. As volunteers in the French army Moroccan soldiers acquired a sense of discipline and a training which made their native courage and endurance effective in modern warfare.

A very great service was rendered to Morocco by French and to a lesser extent by Spanish scholars. These introduced modern methods into the study of Moroccan history, architecture, linguistics, and sociology. They photographed and measured buildings, restored and excavated monuments, and rediscovered and edited lost manuscripts. They also trained Moroccan students to carry on the work which they had initiated.

In all this there was much for which Moroccans had reason to be grateful and for which they did feel gratitude. But there was another aspect to the matter which struck them forcibly. It became clear by degrees that these benefits were incidental to the work of the protectorate. The latter certainly reinvigorated the indigenous life of Morocco, but it did so as a by-product of the effort to give it a neo-French civilization not to re-create Morocco's traditional Muslim and Arab personality. The protectorate, in other words, was tending to make Morocco a part of France, economically, culturally, and politically. No effort was ever made to organize a reformed Sherifian Makhzen. At the end of the forty-four years of the protectorate the same Grand Vizir was in office as at the beginning, though he was now over a hundred years old. An effort by the Sultan to form an imperial cabinet of energetic and independent-minded young men was speedily ended by an ultimatum. The new legal system did not apply generally; the mass of Moroccans were still subject to justice arbitrarily administered by officials who used their powers to serve the political objectives of the protectorate. The educational system was excellent as far as it went; but it was given in French not in Arabic, and while it provided for all European children, it did not extend to more than perhaps one in five of the potential Moroccan school population. It appeared that Morocco was thought of at the best as a future French province; at the worst as a good financial proposition. All this was galling to Moroccans.

At first the shock of the final collapse was so great and the impression of the material superiority of the foreigners so overwhelming, that members of the Makhzen and all except those in the dissident areas (whom lack of contact allowed still to put their trust in traditional methods) bowed their heads and adapted themselves to the new conditions as best they could. As contact with the Europeans increased, they began to perceive that it was possible to acquire the foreign techniques and apply them to Moroccan ends. Soldiers serving in the French army began to pick up French ideas; so did Moroccans in contact with the administration; so did sick people who were treated for the first time by European doctors or nursed in modern hospitals; so did the menservants and the maidservants working in French households and the farm hands working for French settlers. The most profound impression of all was made on the boys who attended modern schools. Parents had at first regarded with horror the suggestion that a Muslim boy should attend an infidel school, while the mere idea of this sort of education for a girl was out of the question altogether. It took a quarter of a century for the attitude to change; but when it did the demand for modern education rapidly increased. Once boys who had received modern education grew up they saw their country's future in a new light. They began to realize that adherence to an outworn way of life had been a main cause of Morocco's downfall. There seemed no reason why the adoption of a modern way of life would not enable them to recover their national individuality as an independent state.

A similar process took place in the Spanish zone, though there were a number of differences, as well as resemblances. While France was hindered by involvement in two World Wars, Spain's task was rendered more difficult by a disastrous civil war. Her zone was relatively small, consisting for the most part of mountainous country which had never been fully under the control of the Makhzen. The Spanish protectorate was planned on the same general lines as the French. The Sultan's Viceroy in Tetuan was given the same show of imperial authority and a Council of Ministers who had no real say in anything. It was from Morocco that the Spanish national rising of 1936 was initiated; its success was due in part to the use of Moroccan troops, an interesting development of Spanish-Moroccan relations recalling the times of Alfonso X. This naturally encouraged the Spanish tendency to a policy in many respects more tolerant than that of the French. Moroccans from the Spanish zone were for example permitted to pursue their studies in the

Middle East, if they so wished, and at one time students were actually despatched there with scholarships. In so far as the supply of teachers permitted, education was given in Arabic and not in Spanish. Apart from the Larache area, there was hardly any attempt to settle Spaniards on the land. As a general rule there was very little co-operation between the two protecting powers and the two zones were administered to all intents and purposes as if they were foreign countries. Outside Tetuan there were no serious disturbances in the Spanish zone after 1926 and the final years of the protectorate passed without any of the troubles which marked the last days of the régime in the south.

The whole history of the protectorate can be divided into four periods. In the first, which extended from 1912 to 1926, Moroccans in the dissident areas continued resistance in the old style, half Holy War and half defence of tribal autonomy, while Moroccans in the areas in which control had passed from the Makhzen to the protectorate powers, realizing the hopelessness of such methods, began to adapt themselves to modern life. The second, from 1926 to 1934, was an intermediate period in which tribal resistance lingered on in the south while politically organized resistance came into being else-where. The third from 1934 to 1944, marked the increase of resistance to French control accompanied by a demand for reforms within the framework of the protectorate. The fourth from 1944 to 1956 saw the formulation and ultimate success of the demand for the restoration of independence.

The prelude to this fourfold development was an immediate hostile reaction in Fez to the signing of the Treaty. It took the form of the massacre of seventy-three French, mostly military, in the course of what came to be known to French writers as *Les Journées Sanglantes de Fès*, followed by a tribal attack on the city. Both these troubles were promptly suppressed. It took rather longer to settle the new relations of the Sultan with his protectors. Maulay Abd al-Hafidh was soon reduced to a state of nervous collapse by the realization of what he had done and of his own and the Makhzen's subsequent impotence. Within four months he had abdicated and prepared to take up residence as a pensioner in Tangier, like Abd al-Aziz, whom he had dispossessed for his failure to resist the foreigner. The brothers remained unreconciled and never again met except one day when they happened to come face to face on their mules and both hurriedly turned back without speaking. The French secured the accession of a third brother, Maulay Yusuf. Maintained in all the traditional pomp of Moroccan sovereigns he proved an admirable choice from the point of view of the new rulers, since his virtue enabled him to retain the respect of his subjects while he co-operated with the real rulers in the way which they wished.

Two leaders from the dissident areas within the French zone attacked the new régime, one from the Taza region, the other from the south; both were finally put out of action in 1917. The attack from the south was the more important. Its leader, al-Hiba, was the son of the famous *murábit*, Ma al-Ainain, who came, like the Almoravids, from Mauritania and left a notable memorial of himself in the buildings which he constructed at Smara in the northern section of the present Spanish Sahara. Al-Hiba's attempt was put down with the help of certain chiefs in the High Atlas of whom the best known was Madani al-Glawi who had been Grand Vizir to Maulay Abd al-Hafidh. These chiefs were rewarded for their services by being allowed to retain and extend the fiefs which they had acquired in the Atlas in the period of the Makhzen's weakness. This was the origin of the power of the later Pasha of Marrakesh, Thami al-Glawi. It was really a breach of the treaty pledge to the Sultan since his security had always required the suppression of such local despots as soon as circumstances permitted.

In the Atlantic and Straits section of the Spanish zone, another problem of the former régime was handed on to the new authorities in the person of the Sherif Ahmad al-Raisuni.

In the days before the protectorate this man's courage, intelligence, ruthlessness, and arrogance, combined with the popular belief in his possession of that mysterious power, *baraka*, had led to his being at one time governor, at another a prisoner of the Makhzen, and at another an outlawed bandit. In the latter capacity he kidnapped successively Maulay Abd al-Aziz's military adviser, Caid Sir Harry Maclean; *The Times* correspondent, Walter Harris; and an American millionaire, for whom he received a ransom of £20,000. A convinced Muslim, with a fanatical belief in his own destiny and that of his people, he was nevertheless ready to co-operate in his own interest with any master. In this he carried on a tradition dating from the last days of the Muslim Christian struggle in Spain. Rosita Forbes took down his story from his own lips. 'Patience is the only thing left to us. Once our race was great . . . now it is your turn to teach. . . . At present you are full of power, but you are spilling it wastefully and Islam is lapping up the drops as they fall. . . . Some day when we have profited by your schools and factories we shall retake what is ours, but it will not be in our life time nor yet in that of our children's children.'[31] Raisuni here miscalculated. Morocco 'took back what was hers' while Raisuni's son Khalid was still Pasha of Larache under the Spanish. Accused, as his father had been, of using his influence with the foreigner for his own profit, he was forced to flee to Spain when independence came, but was included in the amnesty granted by King Hassan on the inauguration of parliamentary life in 1963.

In the first days of the protectorate the Spanish, by appointing Raisuni governor, were able to make use of his great influence in order to instal their own régime. In this capacity he built himself a vast palace at Arzila, hoping ultimately to secure his appointment as the Sultan's viceroy in the whole zone. His ruthless, traditional methods were however more than the local Spanish commander, Colonel Silvestre, who was a bluff, masterful soldier, could stomach. In Raisuni's autobiography there is a vivid description of the scene between the two men when Silvestre paid a surprise visit to Arzila to investigate stories of Raisuni's extortion and the conditions in his prison. On one pretext and another Raisuni put Silvestre off for two hours before he yielded to his insistence and led the way to the prison. The account continues in Raisuni's own words.

'Come in' I said. But he stood there as if his eyes were on sticks which pushed them out of his head. 'God', he said, 'are all the men in the country criminals?' It was a small place, not much bigger than this tent, so that it looked crowded, for there were nearly a hundred prisoners there. To make room, half of them had been fettered to the same chain, and one or two were perhaps dead. . . . It was very dark and nothing could be seen clearly. . . . Do you know when you see twin points of light, and it is a face watching you? So the prisoners watched without moving. . . . Silvestre would have spoken to them, but the smell caught him in the throat and drove him out. He held something across his face. 'This is horrible, inhuman. I will not stand it in a country which is under our protection.'[31]

Silvestre got the men released but Raisuni, unwilling to govern by any means but his own, was soon at war with Spain. His own imprisonment by the Makhzen earlier had been almost equally cruel, but he never complained. It took the Spanish forces eight years to reduce Raisuni to impotence in the hills, and in the end he was captured not by them but by a nobler type of resistance fighter, Mohammed Abdelkrim al-Khattabi.

Addelkrim's father was Caid of the Beni Uriaghel, a Berber tribe in the Rif near Alhucemas. A man of progressive outlook he saw that his sons had a modern education. One was trained as a mining engineer in Spain while the future leader worked in the Spanish office of native affairs in Melilla. Though from a Berber-speaking tribe he was an Arabic scholar and became Chief Cadi of the Melilla area and editor of the local Spanish paper. For some reason he was later imprisoned by the Spaniards. When released he retired to Ajdir and began to organize armed resistance. The former Colonel Silvestre, now General and commanding on the eastern front, gave him his chance when he advanced rapidly westwards without protecting his flanks. The result was a fearful Spanish disaster at Mount Anual in July 1921, when 16,000 men out of a force of 19,000 were killed or taken prisoner, with the loss of virtually all their arms and artillery. With the supplies and prestige thus acquired Abdelkrim created a 'Republic of the Rif' with himself as president. In making his tribe the basis of his government he followed tradition, but in other respects his little republic was given a modern organization. The French Resident General, Marshal Lyautey, was seriously alarmed. He wrote:

Nothing could be worse for our régime than the establishment so near Fez of an independent Muslim state, modernized . . . making Krim a centre of attraction not only for our own dissidents but also for all those Moroccan elements, particularly the young, whose outlook has been broadened by recent events in the east and in whose minds xenophobic aspirations have been raised'.[32]

The young Moroccans concerned would have considered their aspirations patriotic rather than xenophobic, but the Marshal was justified in his fears.

When the French then extended their military occupation into hitherto unoccupied territory adjoining Abdelkrim's area and thus threatened his food supplies, he attacked their outlying posts and involved them in a disaster only second to that suffered by the Spanish. The crisis for once brought the two protectors into close co-operation. While the French under Marshal Pétain, with 325,000 men commanded by eighty generals, attacked from the north, the Spaniards, who had 100,000 men in the field, landed a force at Alhucemas and captured Abdelkrim's village capital at Ajdir. The end soon followed and in April 1926 the heroic five-year struggle was over when Abdelkrim surrendered to the French and was exiled to Reunion. He had shown what resources of energy and courage still existed in the Moroccan people. He was however born out of time. Another ten or twenty years were needed to produce a generation of Moroccans capable of forming the framework of a modern state. When, twenty-one years later, the French decided to allow Abdelkrim to live in France he left the ship at Port Said and took refuge in Egypt. Here he was made head of the Maghrib Office which the nationalists had founded in Cairo. But by now he was totally out of touch and sympathy with the new generation. He died in 1963 having refused to return to Morocco as long as any foreign soldiers remained in North Africa.

The collapse of the Rif Republic did not mark the end of tribal resistance which continued in the Anti-Atlas until 1934. But it did coincide with the moment when the young generation of Moroccans began to think of inaugurating a new type of opposition to the protectorate. This originated not among tough tribesmen in outlying districts but in the cities and among the first graduates from the new schools and their contemporaries in the traditional mosque university in Fez. Just four months after Abdelkrim's surrender, on the night of the first of August 1926, eight young men from Rabat, now the administrative capital of the French zone and two young men from Tetuan, the capital of the Spanish zone, met in the garden of one of them outside the walled city of Rabat. They sat under a mulberry tree, beneath the stars. As they sipped their mint tea they exchanged rumours and became indignant over the ban on the introduction of the Arabic press from Egypt which the French authorities had just imposed. A twenty-five-year-old graduate of the Qarawiyin Mosque University in Fez, who had since been attending lectures in the newly-founded Cairo University, began to tell them about life in Egypt. They listened with interest to his account of the growth of nationalism in the east, of the activities of the Egyptian Wafd and to extracts from the speeches of Zaghlul Pasha. After some time their host, Ahmed Balafrej, who was the youngest of the party, being then eighteen years old, interrupted impatiently to ask the speaker if he was never coming to the point. The latter, a Tetuani, then drew a paper from his pocket and began to read. It was an analysis of the political situation in Morocco and ended with a proposal to form a society to fight maraboutism, to restore the independence of Morocco, and to revive its ancient glory. Just thirty years later that night's host, Ahmed Balafrej, became first Foreign Minister of independent Morocco. In the same year, 1926, a similar meeting of young men students at the Qarawiyin, was held in one of the beautiful, dark, crumbling madrasas of Fez. Here the discussion followed the midday prayer and the eating of a frugal students meal. The leading spirit was another eighteen-year-old, known already as a poet and particularly as author of a patriotic poem beginning:

Am I fifteen already and passing my time in play,
While my people are in bondage and unable to find their way?

His name was Allal al-Fasi and eighteen years later he was to become President of the Istiqlal Party. In the following year the two groups learned of one another's existence and joined forces.

From now on the development of the nationalist independence movement resembles in general outline that of similar movements elsewhere. The first demands put forward were for reform within the framework of the protectorate treaty. In retrospect they sound very reasonable – more schools, the reform of the judicial system, the abolition of the régime of the Grand Caids in the south, study missions in France and the east, the abolition of official colonization, the application to Morocco of French social legislation, and the suppression of licensed prostitution. But the young men, were not taken very seriously. A French colonialist paper referred to them as a 'clique of street urchins who have picked up some vague certificates of study and want to play in Morocco the roll of Gandhis and Zaghluls. Do not they realize', it went on to say, 'that the latter are influential because they are men of conscience, while these boys are nothing but digestive tubes?' By this time it was really unpardonable not to realize the change which was taking place in the minds of the Moroccan people. It was already many years since Lyautey had submitted a famous report on this very subject. In November 1920 he wrote: 'A young generation is growing up, which is full of life and needs activity. . . . Lacking the outlets which our administration offers only sparingly and in subordinate positions, they will find an alternative way out.' His advice was ignored and the way out was found by them more completely and more rapidly than he himself had anticipated.

60 Seven years before the signing of the Treaty of Fez which gave Morocco French protection, the German Kaiser Wilhelm II visited Tangier to demonstrate German support of Moroccan independence.

61 But as subsequent events showed, Germany was one more contending power interested in establishing a claim on Morocco. The Sultan Maulay Abd al-Hafidh was forced to sign the Treaty of Fez in 1912 which gave France the protectorate.

62 Maulay Abd al-Hafidh was succeeded as Sultan by his brother Maulay Yusuf who lived as a traditional Moroccan sovereign.

63 He was an admirable choice from the French point of view because of his effective co-operation. On a visit to Paris in 1929 he was escorted by General Lyautey.

64 The Moroccan delegation at the
Conference of Algeciras in 1906 which
affirmed the integrity and independence
of the Sultan but prepared the way for
French and Spanish control.

65 In the early days of the protectorate
Sherif Ahmad al-Raisuni was appointed
Governor of Arzila in the Spanish zone
but he was an individualist and eventually rebelled. He dictated his autobiography to the English writer Rosita
Forbes (*right*) who published it in 1924.

66 During the protectorate, modern schools were founded where instruction was given in French.

67 One of the many French settlers who came to Morocco, in friendly conversation with a shepherd boy.

68 Nationalist feeling encouraged by the Sultan Mohammed V led to his deposition in 1953. Popular resistance grew and this was one of many hostile demonstrations.

69 Rebellions also broke out due to the breakdown of French authority. This was a scene in the ensuing repression.

70 The Pasha of Marrakesh, Thami al-Glawi was instrumental in securing the deposition of the Sultan Mohammed V by the French.

71 The Palace of the Pasha of Marrakesh in the High Atlas where he exercised independent rule over a vast area.

72 When the Sultan Mohammed V was exiled in 1953, the French replaced him with a nonentity and elderly member of the Royal Family. A demonstration organized by the French in his favour.

73 But feeling amongst the Moroccan people kept growing favouring the return of their exiled sovereign and enthusiasm developed toward idolatry.

74 Al-Glawi realized that there was no chance of securing peace and begged forgiveness from the exiled Sultan in October 1955. The Sultan returned in November of the same year.

75 In the following spring complete independence was recognized. The Sultan was greeted by enthusiastic crowds after signing agreements with France and Spain in 1956.

8   Sovereignty recovered

FOUR THINGS, two native and two foreign, distinguish the national movement in Morocco from those of other countries. The most important though the latest was the great part played by the monarch. Next in importance was the presence of three million Berber-speaking Moroccans and the mistaken interpretation put on this fact by the French authorities. The other two factors, the Act of Algeciras and the division of the country into three zones, were the result of foreign intervention.

Shadowy as the authority of the Act of Algeciras was, it served at the beginning of the protectorate to ensure the theoretical maintenance of the integrity of Morocco. In the last ten years of the protectorate it enabled the US government successfully to challenge certain economic measures taken by the French authorities in Morocco. It limited French and Spanish liberty of economic action because it fixed a common *ad valorem* tariff of $12\frac{1}{2}$ per cent on all imports into Morocco. This prevented the imposition of protective tariffs for Moroccan industries, and did not bar the protecting powers from subjecting the Moroccan economy in their respective zones to their own economies; but it did support the nationalist claim that Morocco was an international question, in respect of which the Spanish and French governments did not enjoy complete freedom of action. The Act permitted other powers besides the two protectors to exercise special privileges on Moroccan territory. The British government maintained a public post office of its own in Fez until almost the end of the protectorate and others in Tetuan and Tangier until its termination. These afforded the nationalists a valuable means of censorship-free communication, a point which the first Moroccan governor of Tetuan after independence mentioned with gratitude at a ceremony when the former post office there was finally converted to other purposes. Though the Act of Algeciras prepared the way for the introduction of Franco-Spanish rule, the action of the Makhzen in securing its meeting helped it in the long run.

The division of Morocco into three zones resulted in the creation of three administrations, differing in methods, language, and economic systems, and the consequent establishment of internal customs and passport barriers. This created a difficult problem of reunification when Morocco regained independence. But the cause of Moroccan nationalism gained far more than it lost. The two protectors rarely saw eye to eye and their differences were generally to the advantage of the third party. In the final years of crisis, refugees from the French zone were able to live and operate in the Spanish zone. A number of boys from Tetuan were able to take advantage of Spanish tolerance in educational matters to study at the Najat School in Nablus during the British Mandate in Palestine and to go on from there to the American University in Beirut or the newly-founded Cairo University. They thus acquired a knowledge of English and Arabic and also of Middle Eastern affairs which was later very useful both to themselves and to their country. In the south the young nationalists were accustomed to look to the political left in Paris for sympathy and when the Spanish nationalist rising took place in 1936 Allal al-Fasi called it a 'Fascist conspiracy'. The Moroccans of the northern zone had on the other hand been bitterly disillusioned with the Spanish leftists during the period of republican government. They therefore regarded Franco's initiative in a different light. With the approval of the Khalifa, tribesmen of the northern zone enlisted in large numbers and played a considerable part in bringing about the nationalist victory. They had their reward in the intensification of the Spanish pro-Arab policy. There can be no doubt that in the end Moroccan nationalism gained much more than it lost from Spanish participation in the protectorate.

The multi-national administration in Tangier, torn as it constantly was by disputes between the various nations concerned, served to facilitate the communications of Moroccan nationalism with the outer world. Under a régime which provided a free money market and facilities for all sorts of shady dealings and shady people, including smugglers, Tangier enjoyed a very marked if spurious economic development, based largely on speculative operations. This enhanced its natural advantages as a tourist centre, caused the city to grow, and provided employment for Moroccans. It is doubtful whether the Moroccan population benefited in other respects from the multi-national régime, and they suffered a serious economic collapse when the artificial advantages were withdrawn and the zone reabsorbed into the national economy.

It was not so much the presence of the three million Berber-speaking Moroccans as the French attitude towards them which caused the first success of Moroccan national sentiment. This arose from the fact that the Berber-speaking population lived in definite geographical localities, mainly in the mountain areas which had been the regions of dissidence before the occupation; they often still observed Berber customary law, and many of them were of a rather European looking physical type. This led many French observers to consider that they must be a minority or be capable of forming a minority in the sense in which the Turks in Cyprus or the Kurds in Iraq form minorities. It was felt that they must bear a grudge against the Arabic-speaking majority and desire to have schools in which instruction was given in Berber. Many French scholars went further and tended, following a tradition which others had already created in Algeria, to present Moroccan history in terms of a prolonged conflict between Arabs and Berbers. There does not seem to be any justification for this. It is easy to find sarcastic Arab reference to Berbers such as the story that Adam, father of mankind, had declared Eve to be divorced when he was told that she was the mother of the Berbers as of the rest of humanity. But in such stories the word Berber seems to be used to describe a rustic, illiterate person rather than a racial or cultural group. The usage is parallel to that of Arab writers such as Ibn Khaldun who on occasions use the word 'Arab' in a pejorative sense, meaning by this simply nomads or peasants. The three great Moroccan Berber dynasties were all anxious to attribute

Arab genealogies to themselves. Ibn Tumart, the Mahdi, who was certainly Berber by origin, himself did this and was so far arabized that his disciple al-Baidaq only discovered after several months intimate association with him that he talked Berber as well as he did Arabic. The fact that Ibn Tumart prepared Berber versions of his teachings, or that Berber-speaking preachers were appointed, was a matter of practical utility and not of nationalist sentiment. However, the protectorate authorities in the French zone having formed their opinion sought to turn the supposed state of affairs to political advantage. 'It is not our business to teach Arabic to populations that have hitherto got on without it', was a saying attributed to Lyautey himself. 'Arabic is a factor of islamization because it is acquired with the Quran. It is our interest to make the Berbers develop outside the framework of Islam.' Lyautey's successors went further than this. A school was set up in Azrou to implement these principles; years later, when nationalism became a force, its students turned out to be just as keen nationalists as any others. In 1930 the Residency induced the young Sultan, who had succeeded Maulay Yusuf three years before, to sign a decree (the Berber Dahir) which was designed to encourage Berber separatism by perpetuating Berber customary law. This presented the nationalists with a cause which was calculated to arouse indignation not only in Morocco but in the whole Muslim world. The matter was publicized by the Pan-Arab leader Shekib Arslan in his paper *La Nation Arabe*, published in Geneva, and the protest echoed and re-echoed throughout the Muslim east. In Moroccan mosques a new petition 'Gracious Lord, deliver us from the blows of destiny and separate us not from our Berber brothers' was recited after the litany, *Ya Latif*. After many months the Dahir was amended, marking the first concession to Moroccan nationalism.

In the Spanish zone no such policy was ever attempted, whether out of greater perceptiveness or because the experience with Abdel-krim had been too clear a lesson.

The first indication that the monarchy might become an ally of nationalism against the protectorate occurred shortly after this episode. Mohammed V (fifth of the Alawite dynasty of that name) had succeeded to his father, Maulay Yusuf, in 1927 at the age of seventeen. Being a third son, he had not been educated for the throne but was selected by the French authorities on account of a retiring disposition which led them to suppose that he would be as amenable to their wishes as his father had been. But he was the contemporary of the generation of young men who were now forming nationalist societies and the affair of the Berber Dahir may well have accentuated an instinctive sympathy with their theses. It was now that they instituted a festival known as the *Fête du Trône*; this was to be celebrated on 18 November each year, the anniversary of the Sultan's accession. In later years, Mohammed V used the occasion to make important political pronouncements whose cautious and diplomatic wording did not prevent them from being often unwelcome to the French authorities. They were suspicious of the implications from the beginning, but they resigned themselves and from the following year, 1934, the celebration was officially recognized. The same year saw both the collapse of the final tribal resistance, south of the Atlas, and the first large-scale manifestation of the new nationalism. In May, when the Sultan paid one of his routine ceremonial visits to Fez, a tumultuous welcome was organized in the course of which various anti-French incidents occurred. The visit was cut short and a communiqué issued, expressing the Sultan's disapproval of 'these regrettable incidents'. Privately he told the nationalists that he had so acted in order to save the people of Fez from possible French reprisals.

For another ten years nationalist propaganda was carried on without overt support from the Sultan. In 1937 there was a major explosion at Meknès when it was suspected that water was being diverted to French settlers at the expense of Moroccan cultivators. There were thirteen dead and a hundred wounded among the demonstrators, while the police and military also suffered casualties. In the subsequent repression Allal al-Fasi, now the recognized leader of the nationalist movement was deported to Gabon where he was detained for nine years. During this time he devoted himself to learning French and to extensive reading. On the basis of the latter he later published a book entitled *al-Naqd al-Dhati* (*Autocriticism*) in which he expounded his views on political and other matters as a basis for discussion by his fellow nationalists.

Following the repression, the authorities introduced a number of minor reforms and the Resident General took the opportunity to issue an admonitory circular to departmental chiefs. In this he stated that the administration was not giving due importance to 'native policy' and that those responsible for it were not able to make the best use of the technical departments. The implication seemed to be that the interests of the Moroccan people, from being the primary interest of government, had become the speciality of a particular service whose needs were apt to be overlooked by busy departmental heads. However the Meknès explosion was followed by two years calm and on the outbreak of war in 1939 the Sultan called for the whole-hearted co-operation of his people with France. A large Moroccan contingent served with distinction in the French army.

The subsequent French collapse, allied propaganda in favour of self-determination, the spread of broadcasting in Arabic, the arrival of Anglo-American forces, and the meeting of the Sultan with President Roosevelt all combined to produce a radical change. The artificial isolation in which Moroccans had been kept since the imposition of the protectorate in 1912 was ended; at the same time the feeling of impotence before the might of France, which had settled upon Morocco when the traditional forms of resistance had collapsed, began to evaporate. In January 1944 after a re-organization of the nationalist movements and the formation of a party with the title 'Istiqlal', meaning independence, a lengthy memorandum was submitted to the Sultan, the French authorities, and the Allies, in which the signatories asked for independence, linked with a democratic constitution. In the following days certain leaders, including Balafrej, now Secretary General of the new party, were arrested on a trumped-up charge of 'intelligence with the enemy' meaning the Nazis. In the disorder provoked by these arrests at least thirty Muslims were killed in Fez. By now the nationalist demand had wide support among the people, at least in the towns.

The lesson was not lost on Mohammed V. He was a born dip-lomat, in whom caution and common sense were linked with a high sense of mission as ruler and as representative of the Alawite dynasty. Deeply religious, he combined adherence to the traditional obser-vances of his faith with a mind open to modern developments. A modest exterior concealed a determined will. From now on until the achievement of independence the major initiatives came from him. In 1947 he persuaded a liberal-minded Resident General to obtain the permission of the French government to visit Tangier, passing through the Spanish zone on the way. Neither zone had been visited by the monarch since the establishment of the Protectorate. The journey was a triumphal procession; in Tangier the Sultan made a speech in which he emphasized the links which bound Morocco to the Arab world while omitting the polite phrase concerning France which it had been understood that he would include. In conse-quence the liberal Resident General was replaced by a soldier, General Juin, of Algerian settler origin. Though the new Resident General inaugurated his proconsulship (and it was the last occasion on which such a term was appropriate in Morocco) with a certain subtlety, he introduced a policy which was to lead in the time of his successor to the deposition of the Sultan and the ultimate collapse of French rule. While making clear that he intended Morocco to remain linked with France, General Juin said that he would himself be a nationalist, if he were a Moroccan. Planning to introduce a kind of Franco-Moroccan co-sovereignty he veiled this in an apparent agreement with the Istiqlal demand for democratic development. In future, municipalities would be elected. The catch in this was that half the Councils in the larger towns were to be French. The Sultan, becoming increasingly assured of the new strength of national feeling, now resorted to the exercise of the one power which he possessed in the legislative field. He began to refuse to append the signature which was essential to make the Resident General's draft decrees legally effective. This provoked a major crisis; for the whole protectorate system had been built on the basis that the Sultan was the sole authority qualified to speak for Morocco and that he could be won over by his desire to conserve his position. In some embar-rassment the French government invited Mohammed V to make a state visit to France, hoping to placate him by compliments and the splendour of his reception. On the contrary, the Sultan took the opportunity to request negotiations for a radical change in Franco-Moroccan relations. He met with a non-committal response, but his action assured him a triumphal reception from his own people on his return to Morocco.

Another crisis followed when General Juin turned out of the Council Chamber an Istiqlal member who criticized the administration. The offender and the ten other elected Moroccan members who all followed him out, were received by the Sultan within an hour. Meanwhile the Glawi, considered the 'friend of France' and representative of what the General was later to describe as the 'real Morocco' (*le Maroc réel*), was being encouraged to defy the Sultan. At a reception in the Palace he told the latter to his face that he was Sultan not of Morocco but of the Istiqlal. Mohammed V had him turned out of the Palace on the spot, and forbade him to return. Having failed to win the Sultan by either compliments or by veiled threats, General Juin now made use of a reproduction of the sort of situation which had brought about the original signing of the protectorate treaty. In February 1951 tribesmen who could not have moved without the acquiesence and encouragement of the French authorities assembled on the outskirts of Rabat. French troops meanwhile surrounded the palace supposedly to protect the Sultan. In view of the menace which he saw threatening him the Sultan yielded to the extent of authorizing the Grand Vizir to issue a vague disavowal of a 'certain political party'. Thereupon tribesmen and French troops were withdrawn. In memoirs which he published some years later General Juin claimed that he had thus brought about a general appeasement. In fact it was reported by correspondents at the time that for days after this operation tribesmen presented themselves at the *Bureaux des Affaires Indigènes* in large numbers, requesting that new Caids should be appointed since they had discovered that they had been led by the existing Caids into an unwitting demonstration against the Sultan. Scepticism as to the genuine nature of the affair was freely expressed in France as well as by liberal-minded Frenchmen in Morocco. A few weeks after the event the Sultan himself informed an Egyptian journalist that he had acted under duress and did not feel bound by his statement.

When a few months later General Juin was transferred to a high command in Europe, he succeeded in inducing the French government to appoint General Guillaume as his successor. The latter followed a similar policy with less subtlety. Soon after his arrival he was quoted as saying that he would 'make the nationalists eat straw'. From now indeed it seemed as if policy in Morocco was determined neither by the government in Paris nor by the Residency but by shadowy figures in the background, officials and businessmen, with the longdistance support of the late Resident General, now promoted Marshal. In January 1952 a nationalist meeting of protest in Casablanca was made the occasion for arresting hundreds of Istiqlal leaders. Detained in prison for two years they were released on the appointment of a new Resident General 'for lack of evidence'. Taken in conjunction with the previous dispersion of Istiqlal leaders, who were seeking foreign sympathies abroad, this was a blow from which the organization never recovered. In the meantime local control passed to more revolutionary and less experienced men. On the French side preparations now began for a repetition of the 1951 manœuvre on a much grander and more methodical scale. This time it was intended to remove Mohammed V from the scene altogether. The operation does not seem to have been the work of any one person or group of people. It was rather a matter of an unspoken understanding between influential officials and French residents who shared the same outlook. The idea was to stage a demonstration by what Marshal Juin called the 'real Morocco'. This was to be presented as a spontaneous rising of the Moroccan people against a hated political party and against the Sultan who had sold himself to them. There were in fact many Moroccans who supported the French connexion, some from conviction that Morocco was still unable to stand by herself but many more because their own position depended on this connexion. First and foremost among these was Thami alGlawi, Pasha of Marrakesh, who was well aware that one of the first actions of any independent Moroccan government would be to put an end to his tyranny in the vast area in which he assumed the airs of a semiindependent prince. In French eyes the

Glawi had been built up as the incarnation of the 'real Morocco' and Marshal Juin was active in building his reputation up further – as he did at a famous session of the French Academy. Associated with the Glawi was the Sherif Abd al-Hayy al-Kittani, of Fez. The latter was a man of eminence and of great traditional learning, but he was disliked by the nationalists as a reactionary, and as a self-seeking head of a confraternity.

Jointly these two men, with the tacit assent of the administration, began to organize public opposition to the Sultan and to the Istiqlal whom they dubbed jointly as 'communists'. In their mouths this was simply a term of abuse; it indicated any person whose ideas ran counter to the traditions and practices by which they themselves profited and on which their fortune had been built up. They even adopted as their own the 750-year-old charge of Ibn Tumart against the Almoravid princesses and Ali ibn Tashfin, claiming that Mohammed V was a bad Muslim because he had had his daughters, as well as his sons, educated, and allowed them to go about unveiled and take part in public life. Since it was believed that the sympathies of the administration were with them, the two men were able to muster an impressive following, including their own dependants and all those Moroccan officials and others who feared the results of independence. While neither the French government nor the Residency gave any signs of acting with resolution or possessing a definite policy, the conspirators toured the country, collecting signatures, administering oaths, and finally demanding the deposition of the Sultan, and his replacement by a pious but almost unknown and elderly member of the royal family. On 17 August 1953 the Glawi launched his ultimatum:

This is not the moment to mince words. The Moroccan people no longer recognize the Sultan.... We who represent tradition, good faith and the future of this country, want to put the French government on their guard. It faces a terrible responsibility. If, contrary to our expectation, it dare not show the firmness which the Moroccan people expect of it, France will lose her place in Morocco.

The next day, after a spate of contradictory and unimplemented orders from Paris, French troops surrounded the palace and deported the Sultan and his family, first to Corsica and then to Madagascar.

The French fomentors of this plan sincerely believed that they had thus made Morocco safe for France for another twenty years. 'This is a great victory', wrote a French paper in Casablanca, 'gained by the supporters of solid and lasting Franco-Moroccan friendship. From now on nothing will hinder the soaring of hearts and spirits among the inhabitants of this country.'

For a few days there was indeed a stunned calm; but it did not last long. The elderly Sultan was a nonentity. His life was attempted on the first occasion that he attended Friday prayer. After a second attempt he virtually never left his palace in Rabat. The long suspended decrees were signed at last, but no good came of them. The *Fête du Trône* was officially abolished, on the grounds that it was a non-religious festival and therefore illegitimate in a Muslim country. Soon something previously unheard of in Morocco was taking place. Moroccan terrorists began to assassinate Frenchmen and the Moroccans who co-operated with them. French counter-terrorists began to assassinate not only Moroccan nationalists but also liberal Frenchmen. Among Moroccans enthusiasm for the deposed Sultan rose to near idolatry; women believed that they saw his face in the moon. In November 1954 the rising in Algeria made the French position far more difficult; all available forces had to be concentrated in an attempt to save the nominally French province of Algeria. The attitude of the Spanish government was another complication. They had seen no reason to endorse the deposition of the Sultan, about which they had not been consulted, and of which they did not approve. In the northern zone prayer was still said in the name of Mohammed V and the Spanish High Commissioner allowed a monster meeting to be organized to denounce the French action.

In early summer 1955 the French government decided on a complete change of policy and sent to Morocco a determined Resident General with authority to carry out a resolutely liberal new deal. These belated efforts at conciliation were sabotaged by unwilling French officials; the Resident General was hissed and insulted when he attended the funeral of French victims of a bomb outrage. He failed to get his proposals approved in Paris by the date he set, and the result, on the second anniversary of the deposition, was a bloody massacre of Frenchmen by tribesmen at Wadi Zem, which led to his recall. The French government now called a conference of Moroccans representative of all tendencies, including the nationalists, to discuss Morocco's future. The new official proposal was to replace the puppet sovereign with a Crown Council. The agreement of the exiled Sultan was secured to this, but it then took weeks to induce the aged occupant of the throne to retire as a pensioner to Tangier, as Maulay Abd al-Aziz and Maulay Abd al-Hafidh had done before him. By the time he yielded, a Moroccan guerrilla liberation army began to operate against French posts on the Rif and made it clear that nationalist activities were by now far from being under any central control. On 26 October al-Glawi himself destroyed the last chance of France's avoiding a complete surrender. Realizing that he had lost, and wishing to save whatever might be saved for himself and his family, he issued a statement that the Crown Council was illegal: 'I associate myself with the wish of the Moroccan people for the prompt restoration of Sidi Mohammed ibn Yusuf and his return to the throne. This return is the only thing able to restore harmony to men's hearts and spirits.' By 31 October Sidi Mohammed had been recalled to France. The Pasha of Marrakesh sought permission to be received by him in his French hotel. There, approaching on his knees, he kissed the Sultan's robe and his feet and asked for pardon. 'Do not speak to me any more of the past', replied Mohammed V, 'it is the future that matters and it is on your future actions that you will be judged.' On 6 November a meeting between the Sultan and the French Foreign Minister was followed by a communiqué announcing that His Majesty the Sultan of Morocco had confirmed his intention of constituting a Moroccan government to carry on affairs and to negotiate. The communiqué went on:

The mission of this government will in particular be to elaborate institutional reforms for the purpose of making Morocco a democratic state with a constitutional monarchy and to conduct negotiations with France destined to make Morocco acquire the status of an independent state united to France by permanent links of a freely consented and defined interdependence.

The declaration was signed and Mohammed V returned to Morocco on 18 November 1955, the 28th anniversary of his accession.

During the 'Three Glorious Days' which followed, and the subsequent weeks, all Morocco, as it seemed, flowed into Rabat to honour their homecoming sovereign. Extraordinarily few incidents marred the universal rejoicing. Those Moroccans and Frenchmen who were deeply committed by the events of the last few years had absented themselves from the country; the remainder, including the French officials of the administration, adapted themselves to the new situation with remarkably good grace. The Sultan formed a Moroccan government representative of the various tendencies; the French directors of departments were replaced by Moroccans with the rank of ministers.

On 2 March 1956 a new convention recognized the full independence of Morocco including the right to its own foreign service and its own army. The face-saving reference to interdependence in the earlier agreement was now interpreted as implying little or nothing more than the normal relations between two friendly states. On the 7 April 1956 a parallel agreement was signed with the Spanish government. This was followed by a visit of the Sultan, his sons, and most of the ministers, to the former Muslim territories of southern Spain, where the Almoravids and Almohads had once held sway. For the first time for over 700 years a reigning Moroccan Sultan entered the great Mezquita at Cordoba.

On 29 October 1956 the international Statute of Tangier was abrogated; this was followed by the abandonment of the last privileges derived from the Act of Algeciras and from other pre-occupation treaties.

With the recovery of independence, the former *Sadr al-Aatham* or Grand Vizir, Si Mohammed al-Moqri, Grand Vizir before the protectorate and throughout the whole forty-four years of its duration, having seen his country recover its independence, was himself taken to the mercy of God, at the age of 105 years.

Independence had in the end come very much sooner than even the most optimistic nationalist had expected. This had the advantage of avoiding a prolonged struggle which might have involved much greater bitterness than was actually the case. It had the disadvantage that independence came when Morocco was still pitifully short of professional men, of teachers, and of technicians. Of some 1,000 doctors in the country not more than 50 were Moroccans – and of these some had to be withdrawn from the practice of medicine to serve as ambassadors. Eight years later 7,000 foreign experts were still employed by the departments and some 7,000 teachers in the schools.

Nevertheless, the newly-formed government made a good job of the take-over. Moroccan ministers took over from the foreign heads of departments. Moroccan Caids took over from French *Contrôleurs Civils* and from Spanish *Interventores* with a minimum disturbance to public order. A disciplined and well-trained army was rapidly formed from Moroccan troops who had been serving with the French and Spanish armies; the Sultan's eldest son, Maulay Hassan, who was to be named Crown Prince a year later, became Chief of Staff. The absorption of the Liberation Army was more difficult; for some months elements, out of control of the government, made sporadic attacks upon French or Spanish outposts in the south or in Ifni. In the end most of them were successfully integrated into the Royal Forces, an operation in which the Crown Prince took an important part. The economic integration of the former Spanish zone was completed within two years and in 1959 a Moroccan currency based on the dirham (roughly equivalent to a new franc) was introduced for the whole country. Tangier was given a period of grace before having to surrender its profitable financial autonomy. This anomaly had to go and the change resulted in the disappearance of the last internal customs barriers; but so far no means has been found to restore the city's prosperity to its former level. Agreements were negotiated for the progressive withdrawal of French and Spanish troops and of the American airmen from bases which had been introduced by agreement with the French, in the cold-war period, without any reference to the Sultan.

Varying degrees of success were achieved in spheres in which the nationalists had severely criticized the protectorate régime. A vigorous campaign resulted in a speedy multiplication of schools and the scholarization of immensely increased numbers. It was however not so easy to multiply teachers; classes had to be enlarged, hours reduced. One set of children were taught in the morning, another in the afternoon. Still less was it possible to change over to Arabic as the language of instruction since there were neither teachers nor textbooks for this. A limited number of hours of instruction in Arabic was the most that was possible. Nevertheless there was a marked increase in Arabic newspapers and publications. A university was created in Rabat and the number of students of medicine and science greatly increased. In Fez the traditional Qarawiyin Mosque University was converted to a more modern type of institution with secondary and primary schools depending on it. In the field of law, executive and administrative functions were at last separated and a unified legal system introduced for all. The task of replacing shanty towns by decent housing was taken over from the protectorate authorities and developed on the lines already established. The Public Works Department admirably maintained the excellent road system in the south and brought it up to the same standard in the former northern province. New roads have been made to areas of touristic interest, where improved government rest houses have been provided, as well as to villages. Legalized prostitution was abolished immediately and the vast *quartiers reservés*, constructed under the protectorate, were converted to housing estates.

Less success was achieved in the sphere of industry and planned investment. The phenomenal growth of Casablanca after World War II had in part been due to local conditions in France which stimulated French investment in suitable areas outside France itself. Besides the cessation of this factor, the coming of independence, with the consequent fear of labour demands, of nationalization, and of possible difficulties in transferring profits to France resulted in withdrawal of capital and a drop in investment which it has not been possible to make up. Industry has been maintained, but there has been little expansion. A project for developing a ship-building industry at Alhucemas or at Tangier has not materialized. Only after much delay is the giant chemical plant at Safi moving towards the stage of realization, while the scheme for a steel-works near the Algerian frontier, using anthracite from the southern and iron ore from the northern zone, encountered even greater difficulties.

Great hopes were placed in the drawing up of a Ten Years Plan. While the effort resulted in the collection of useful statistics, it finally became clear that the Moroccanized administration did not have the technical competence necessary to assess and carry out the projects considered. Unexpended credits tended instead to be devoted to the scheme known as the *Promotion Nationale* which is particularly connected with the name of King Hassan II. This was intended to mobilize the masses of Moroccan unemployed or underemployed for the execution of projects which would themselves create further employment. Happy evidences of its effects are to be seen in new village schools, in the maintenance of roads and tracks and their extension, in the restoration of monuments, and in the embellishment of towns. The *Promotion Nationale* has nevertheless increasingly taken on the aspect of relief work, pure and simple, rather than that of the investment of labour in projects capable of creating new sources of employment. In Morocco as in all under-developed countries with a high birth-rate this is a problem of major importance. In spite of continued aid from France and new aid from the US and elsewhere, it has not been easy to balance the budget.

A question which was not tackled until the end of 1963 was the recuperation of the agricultural land brought to a high state of efficiency by European colonists. The transfer in itself presents no great difficulty but the problem is how to keep up the standards of cultivation. It is proposed that the large estates shall be maintained as units and managed by the *Office Nationale d'Irrigation*, in the case of irrigated land and by the *Office Nationale de la Modernisation Rurale* in other cases, but here Morocco comes up against the lack of trained technical experts and supervisors which is a problem in every sphere of Moroccan activity.

In the first flush of independence two major projects, calculated to fire the popular imagination, were elaborated. One was the making of the 'Unity Road'. This was to provide a link between Fez and the Mediterranean by connecting the road at Taounate in the former southern with that at Ketama in the former northern zone.

It was to be built 'inexpensively', across mountainous country, by volunteer labour from all parts of the country. In the morning the volunteers worked with pick and shovel; in the afternoons and evening they attended lectures and entertainments in which citizens from the south got to know those from the north and those from the east of the country made acquaintance with those from the west. The scheme was the child of the fertile brain of Mehdi ben Barka, then President of the National Assembly. The other scheme, 'Operation Ploughing', was also undertaken in 1957, and continued for three years. One thousand tractors were assembled and set to plough 375,000 acres of land. Artificial fertilizers were applied to the areas ploughed and the exploitation was divided into two rotations, one for cereals and one for a root break. The work was carried out on land cultivated by Moroccan peasants in order to demonstrate to them the advantages of using modern machinery and modern fertilizers and of treating agricultural land as a large unit. In order to strengthen the impression upon the peasants, the first tractor on each of the three zones was driven by King Mohammed V himself.

Both projects achieved partial, though not complete success; the road-making abilities of the volunteers, for example, besides being less efficient than those of the Public Works Department, also proved in the long run a good deal more expensive. In the case of 'Operation Ploughing' success was limited partly by peasant suspicion of innovations, partly by the real difficulties in which the change of system involved them, partly by the veiled opposition of large owners who suspected the project to be a step towards socialism, and partly by administrative shortcomings due to the lack of trained officials. Three years later the early enthusiasm had waned and official energies were confined to routine administration.

In 1957 Mohammed V changed his style as ruler from Sultan to King, thus symbolizing the intention to introduce a more modern type of government. He also appointed a National Consultative Assembly. Though nominated and not elected this was thoroughly representative and was presided over by the energetic Mehdi ben Barka. For two years it performed a useful work in examining ministerial activities. By the end of 1960 new administrative areas had been delimited which were based on economic instead of on tribal considerations and elections had been held for regional and municipal councils to represent them.

The entirely unexpected death of Mohammed V in February 1961, after a minor operation, was felt in Morocco as an irreparable loss, since his experience and prestige had been regarded as a guarantee of Moroccan stability during the years of adjustment. The Crown Prince who assumed the title of Hassan II behaved with resolution and discretion and announced his intention to continue his father's policy and to fulfil the latter's promise to promulgate a constitution by the end of 1962. In fact a draft was issued by the promised time and ratified in a plebiscite a few weeks later by an overwhelming majority. Though the Constitution was, as the King said 'made with his own hands', and reserved control to the sovereign, it established a parliament of two houses of which the lower is elected by universal suffrage of both sexes. The second house is chosen to the extent of two-thirds by the members of the regional and municipal councils and to the extent of one-third by the chambers of commerce and industry, agriculture and handicrafts.

The first parliament, elected in 1963, assembled on 18 November of that year. When it is realized that Morocco had had no previous experience of self-government or of elections, the rate of advance may be judged to have been as rapid as was reasonable. A majority of Moroccans would probably agree, but the desire of the more radical of the political parties for more speedy democratization has created a latent crisis which we will consider later.

In the field of foreign policy, Moroccan actions have generally been marked by moderation and by a desire to solve disputes by compromise. Thus relations with France have at no time been as strained as Tunisian relations sometimes were, co-operation with French experts within the country has remained friendly, and a relatively high proportion of French and Spaniards have retained their positions in business and other spheres. The most unhappy episode resulted from the kidnapping of five Algerian leaders at the end of 1956 by the French intelligence services when they were travelling in a plane chartered by the Moroccan government, as guests of Mohammed V. An explosion of popular feeling resulted in the murder of a number of French in the Meknès area. Suitable measures were at once taken by the Moroccan government and no rupture followed. Nor was French financial aid ever cut off. Morocco was one of the first countries whose troops participated in the Congo operation in which they gained credit for their conduct in restoring order in the port of Matadi. As a member of the Arab League, Morocco has as far as possible avoided involvement in Arab quarrels. While giving full support to Algeria during the rising, short of actual war, she always stopped short of a complete break with France.

Only in relation with the claim to Mauritania and the frontier question with Algeria has Moroccan moderation been queried by outside observers. These issues have historical bases which require special consideration. Moroccan initiative in forming the Casa/blanca group of states was probably less an expression of permanent Moroccan sympathies in foreign relations than a desire to gain support in the matter of Mauritania and possibly to cut the ground from under the feet of the left/wing opposition within Morocco itself. Morocco never seemed a very comfortable partner in the group and the extent to which any practical co/operation has resulted has been negligible.

Looking as a whole at developments in Morocco since the achieve/ment of independence, we see that there has been a distinct move towards the establishment of a constitutional régime but that there has been no fundamental change in social organization or in the system of administration beyond the substitution of Moroccan for French and Spanish officials. Though the throne retains supreme authority, political parties have been able to exist, to control party presses, and to express their view with a liberty which has often bordered on licence. Strongly implanted in the urban centres, these parties are now actively seeking recruits in the country districts with which they were unable to make much contact before the coming of independence. It is doubtful whether in the mountain and remoter

country areas there is any great interest in the professed party pro-
grammes. In spite of rumblings in the industrial areas, the revolutionary spirit of many students, and some economic difficulties,
Morocco as a whole presents an appearance of relative stability and
indeed prosperity compared with other emergent states.

76 This was the cabinet King Mohammed V formed in 1958 which included Hajj Ahmed Balafrej (*right of king*) and Abdurrahim Bouabid (*left of king*).

77 In 1961 Morocco took the initiative in calling the Casablanca Conference which resulted in the formation of the Casablanca group of African states.

78 and 79   Two of the major projects inaugurated after independence were 'Operation Ploughing' which aimed at cultivating over 300,000 acres, and the building of 'Unity Road' which aimed to provide a link between Fez and the Mediterranean. The King drove the first tractor (*above*) and his son Prince Hassan (*below*) stripped to participate in the road-building.

80 The Bin el Ouidane dam which was inaugurated in 1955 permits irrigation of 250,000 acres of land and is still being developed.

81 The port of Casablanca which owes its foundation to General Lyautey today symbolizes the prodigious development of the economy of modern Morocco. Over ten million tons of merchandise are handled annually.

82 This Moroccan woman is packing sardines for export.

83 The large Samir oil refinery at Mohammedia (Fedala) (*above right*).

84 Cars on the production line at a factory in Casablanca.

85, 86 and 87   The traditional crafts of Morocco such as basket making (*above*), pottery (*below left*) and carpet making (*below right*) are still extensively practised.

88 The old traditional methods are still being used for agriculture as well as the modern equipment.

89 The tanning of leather has long been a craft of the Moroccans; and more modern methods are now replacing traditional equipment as shown here.

90 In February 1961 King Mohammed V died unexpectedly and was succeeded by his son who took the title Hassan II, shown here in the foreground as Prince Hassan.

91 Modern practice and ancient tradition side-by-side is clearly evident in present-day Morocco. King Hassan II rides to the Friday prayer ceremony in traditional style and costume.

9   Morocco today and tomorrow

MOROCCO'S POPULATION must be nearing 12 million. The country has considerable agricultural and mineral resources. Geo-graphy and history have given it close links not only with Africa, but also with the Middle East and Europe. It has a frontage facing America. Less favoured nations may well envy the privileged position of a country which used until recent times to style itself the Fortunate Empire.

The Moroccan people, as we have seen, have had an Islamic past of distinction, including a period of imperial splendour. This was followed by a long eclipse which resulted in their entering the twen-tieth century with a medieval social organism in a state of extreme decay. The intensive action of the protectorate over forty-four years, the stimulation of Moroccan energies which it promoted, and the effects of the general renaissance of the Arab world have been such that today no Moroccan wishes to choose any path other than that common to all modern peoples. Within this Moroccan community, which has a marked individuality as a whole, there are still wide differences between the component elements.

At the top of the social scale we find the royal house, with the many families which have a long tradition of service with the Makhzen. Associated with them, particularly in such cities as Fez, Tetuan, and Rabat, there are a number of well-to-do merchant families, with men of learning and religion. Although the influence of the latter is no longer comparable to what it was before the protectorate it is still important. The upper levels of society have never been closed to arrivals from lower strata. It was always possible for any Moroccan, even a slave when such a class existed, to rise to the highest posts. Since independence there have been ministers who have come from what we should call the working class, thanks entirely to their industry and intelligence. In spite of the recent penetration by European culture, basically Christian or agnostic, Moroccan society still represents the traditions and outlook of that western Muslim and Arab civilization which reached its zenith in Andalusia from the tenth to the thirteenth centuries when it was probably the most advanced in the western world outside Byzantium. From it Moroccans have inherited a refinement of manners, different from those of Europe, which is highly attractive, and an aesthetic appreciation of life, together with a certain distaste for the rush and mechanization of the modern world. In government the individual and his personal relationships still have first importance, diplomacy is the main instrument, and occasional violence the remedy for abuses which are found intolerable.

The modern outlook of French intellectuals imposed on Moroccan minds by the action of the protectorate has resulted in a psychic dualism. This gives rise to many difficult problems of adjustment and is reflected in the outward forms of life. Nothing is more striking than the extraordinarily different impression made by the King himself when dressed in modern European costume, or in army uniform, from that which he makes when he appears as a hieratic figure, on his way from palace to mosque to attend the Friday prayer. In the first case he could be a young Frenchman or American; in the second he seems to have stepped out of a Byzantine mosaic. This contrast between tradition and the twentieth century recurs in every sphere of life. It reveals itself in the architecture of the towns and even in individual buildings. In Casablanca the old town has been completely submerged, and today is little more than a small slum lost in a modern city. In some places however tradition has reasserted itself in 'neo-Moroccan' quarters where interesting experiments were made during the protectorate in the attempt to incorporate the amenities required in modern life into a residence of the old interior type. In Rabat, the ancient town remains distinct from the modern. While the latter is by now far larger, the former retains dignity and vitality. In Fez, the old city is much more impressive than the new; except for the fact that it is beginning to spread outside its walls and that a few houses, even in the old sections, have now a window or two to the exterior, it has almost entirely preserved its original aspect. It is sometimes possible to find a house where a wealthy owner has combined the old and the new in one building. One portion will be of European style, have external windows, and be furnished with high tables and chairs; another portion will be built like a Beni Merin house around an interior court, with its orange trees and fountain, on to which the long narrow rooms, with their delicate plaster-work and their painted woodwork with floral and geometric designs, look out through elegant wrought-iron grills. Meals may vary in the same way; on one occasion food may be served in the European manner to be taken with knives and forks, and on another in the Arab style to be taken with the fingers direct from the traditional bowls. Many Moroccan men sometimes appear in traditional and sometimes in European clothes. The fact that Moroccan ladies also now expect to be provided with costumes of both types imposes a serious extra expense on prospective husbands and is one cause of later marriages.

This difficult process of adaptation, more acute in Morocco than in most other Arab countries, because it occurred there more rapidly, extends through all classes of society. In the cities the old craft organization is passing away with increasing rapidity and will soon be only a memory. In centres such as Casablanca there is now a working-class proletariat, amounting in all to about 250,000. These are mainly uprooted peasants from distant areas of plain or mountain. Arriving without preparation for city life, without technical skills, and often illiterate, they tend to settle in gigantic shanty towns on the outskirts of the cities. Lacking all amenities and often terrible as these are, particularly in the mud of winter or in the great heat of summer, the bidonvilles house a population which is remarkably orderly. Even in these unfavourable circumstances, the artistic instinct of the people often finds expression in little arches and other traditional ornamentation which they manage to give to the tiny Quranic schools or the zawiyas which they improvise from old packing cases or other chance materials. Together with the workers in the mining districts, these factory workers form the mass of recruits for the important trade union movements. Until independence the unions which were illegal, but tolerated towards the end of the protectorate, were largely directed to the achievement of the aims of nationalism. Since then the leaders of the *Union Marocaine de Travail* (UMT) which is much the most important of these organizations tends to devote itself exclusively to class interests and to seek its models in communist or near-communist controlled societies rather than in the west. After 1961 it drew apart from the *Union Nationale des Forces Populaires* (UNFP), its former close ally, the latter being concerned primarily with national politics. Not all this labour force is permanently urbanized; large numbers of Berbers from the south leave their families behind in the country and return home to them after a period of factory life.

Though there are pleasant little townships in the coastal plain, set among orange trees, with mosque and generally attractive surroundings, many of the villages and *douars* of this Arabic-speaking area, consisting of houses of mud or wattle, encircled by cactus, have a desolate and bare appearance, though a newly-constructed school often gives a welcome indication of coming change. The population is seen at its most animated in the weekly markets whose sites are denoted by such names as Suq al-Arba or Suq al-Khamis ('Wednesday Market' or 'Thursday Market'); sometimes these are villages but often simply an open locality where pedlars set up their booths on the appointed day and villagers come from miles around to sell their produce, acquire household necessities, and exchange news. Far larger and more spectacular crowds assemble for the annual *moussems* or festivals held at some saint's sanctuary. These are sometimes on a vast scale, bringing together a concourse of many thousands and are the occasion for folk dancing, powder-play, and other diversions which may last for several days.

In the mountain areas, buildings tend to be of a more solid nature. At such a centre as Tafraout, in the heart of the Anti-Atlas, the dwellings give an air of considerable well-being and are remarkably picturesque. The way of life of the inhabitants in the mountains is very different from that of the cities or of the coastal plain where the people had long been subject to the vicissitudes of rule by the pre-protectorate Makhzen.

In districts where the Berbers before the protectorate lived in dissidence they used to conduct their affairs in various ways which can best be described as primitive forms of democracy. In the Atlas they tended to form rudimentary tribal republics composed of groups of villages. These acknowledged an annual elected chief and met in popular assemblies to discuss important issues. But the mountain areas resembled the plains in the respect paid to holy personages whether hereditarily so, as sherifs, or having acquired the status by their own merits. Such persons would act as mediators, supervise elections, and on occasion assume the role of political leaders. It was said of the famous Abu Mahalli, who managed to replace Maulay Zidan as ruler in Marrakesh for a while in the seventeenth century that he 'began as a saint and ended as a devil'. Reproached for this at a public reception by a simple but devout personage, Abu Mahalli confessed his error and wept. 'We set out to restore religion', he said, 'and we have destroyed it.'

These anarchic little democracies were always liable to collapse under the encroachments of ambitious individuals who locally assumed the authority of a Sultan without being bound by the sanctions which always limited the latter's actions to some extent. Of this process the career of Thami al-Glawi, Pasha of Marrakesh under the protectorate, was an outstanding example; on account of the French protection which he enjoyed his period of power was abnormally long. Today control by the central administration has put an end, presumably for ever, both to dissidence and to the ephemeral triumphs of local despots. Under the protectorate, real authority was exercised locally by a French controller, while the Makhzen was represented by a local notable who generally belonged to the older generation and often spoke only the local language. Since independence the two functions have been combined, and the post is held by a Moroccan of the new type who will almost certainly be at home in French as well as in his mother-tongue. But the cynical attitude to all government and to the people of the towns, acquired through the centuries, will long persist. 'Poet and judge and sheikh are all the same', says a Berber adage ' – after the money of those they meet.' Today the political party organizer, now active in plain and mountain, is no doubt included in the list. In such areas the choice of membership of a party is likely to be decided by its utility as a connexion with the source of patronage and fountain-head of material advantage in the capital rather than by approval of its professed programme.

The mountain people have great vitality and endurance. During World War II they demonstrated proof of their military qualities in France and in Italy. General Guillaume who conducted many campaigns against the Atlas tribes in the course of the conquest described the Berber as the best fighter in North Africa. 'Brave to rashness, he is ready to sacrifice his goods, his family and – much more readily – his life to defend his liberty.' They have a strong, though primitive, artistic sense. This expresses itself in the beauty and diversity of the many types of carpets and rugs which they weave, each in a definite area; in the wealth of folk dances in which both sexes participate; and in a style of architecture of their own.

Original in character and often grandiose, the *tighremts* (fortified villages or houses) are entirely different from the architecture of the towns. Built of beaten earth, often mixed with straw, their square towers thickening at the base, they raise the sober geometric patterns of their decoration towards the firmament. From a comparison with Sudanese architecture it has been suggested that Berber architecture has been influenced by negro art. It appears however that the contrary is true and that nomad Berbers carried with them, right across to the other shore of the desert, the eagle's nest type of buildings in which they stored their grain. For many of these fortress-like buildings are in fact *agadir* or fortified collective granaries.[33]

The Berbers have no tradition of writing either verse or prose, but the Berber spirit is expressed in poems some of which have been collected in the south-western area of the Atlas by the French Colonel Justinard.[34] In them the Berber sense of beauty appears, combined with an earthy common sense, a respect for learning, and a typical respect and sense of awe in the presence of a holy personage.

When God shared beauty out, there were ten received a portion.
Soap, henna, *and silk made three.*
With the plough, flocks, and swarms of bees, they made six.
The sun when he rises on the mountains was the seventh.
The crescent moon, when she is slender as the Christian's dagger,
Horses, and books, brought the count to ten.
What remained was all carried off by Muhammad, the Apostle.

The *henna* mentioned here is a plant which yields a reddish colouring matter used by women and men for dyeing hair and by women for designing patterns on their hands and feet.

There is also a more worldly variant on the same theme.

Beauty – God divided it. Three carried it off.
One portion, the Sun when he rises on the mountains;
Another, the Moon when she rises on the mountains;
The third portion – who carried it off?
Who but the little Ruqiya, the queen of maidens.
   He who has beauty, knowledge, and a fine horse
   Can think he's reached heaven, without passing through the tomb.

Besides cultivators, there are many transhumant Berber tribes whose flocks browse on the high pasturage in summer but descend to the lower levels in the winter.

   When the guardian of the flock dies, who weeps?
   None but the little kid whom he helped a hundred times.

This open-air life on the mountains, with the ocean often not far away is the antithesis of the cloistered interior life of the traditional Muslim town; and Berber verse is at the opposite pole from the sophisticated charm of the literary circles which follow the Arab traditions of Andalusia.

   The boat, if it lie on its side for centuries,
   Will ride on the waves again if it be set upright.
   Everything in the world has a doctor to set it to rights –
   Only for Love and for Death there is no remedy.

In the valleys of the rivers flowing down the southern slopes of the Atlas, and in the pre-Saharan oases, are to be found the finest examples of the villages which the Arabs call *ksur* (singular *ksar*). These are fortified agglomerations in which the houses are so closely packed together, and the streets (which are often tunnels under the first floor of a house) are so narrow, that the effect is of a honeycomb or an irregular wasps' nest. The contrast between the bare hillside and the valley is striking. At levels of four or five thousand feet, the irrigated vegetable gardens are often shaded by great walnut trees; at lower levels these are replaced by palms. The oasis of Tafilalet, with Erfoud and Rissani, has half a million date-palms and supports some 220,000 inhabitants.

All these varying populations have for centuries acknowledged the spiritual and, when compelled to do so, also the temporal authority of the Sultan and have thus always had the sense of belonging to the Moroccan community.

Modern means of transport, the central control introduced under the protectorate, and the spread of broadcasting and education, have all brought closer together the various elements of the population. The struggle for independence, symbolized by the deposition and restoration of Mohammed V, gave them a new cohesion. Today the future of Morocco depends on the extent to which the urban *élite* can rise to the task of leadership of the former dissident areas.

The presence of the Mediterranean on the north and the Atlantic on the west, with the desert on the south and the difficult mountain approach on the east, make Morocco a sort of terminus in which human immigrants and religious, political, and artistic, influences arrive after a long journey and come to rest. There is virtually no through traffic in ideas. Today national sentiment and the striving for a materially renovated world are taking the place of religion as a driving force. It remains to be seen whether in Morocco these can generate in today's leaders the sense of urgency and purpose which will enable them to achieve the great results which religious impulse brought about in the case of the Almoravids and the Almohads.

Made part of Africa by a geographical accident, Morocco is at the same time all but part of Europe. Yet the feature which determines its character most decisively is the fact that it forms the western extremity of the vast, desert-interspersed, area which extends from the Indus to the Atlantic. This has caused the country to be indelibly marked by Islam and the Arabic language so that it is properly numbered among the Arab lands. Those who know the other states of the Arab League can form an idea of Morocco without having ever been there. The resemblances include the outer forms of life, religious practices, the position of women, the language of press and literature, the dangers of drought and of locusts. Morocco will always share, even if in a somewhat detached manner, the outlook of the eastern Arab states in matters of general Arab interest, including the Arab determination to restore the dispossessed people of Palestine to their homeland. As in the Arab states, Zionist propaganda is a source of unrest and is officially banned. But while cherishing membership of the Arab League, Morocco will avoid involvement in Arab controversies which do not directly concern her.

Her position in the Far West, and the mountainous character of much of the country, have combined to make Morocco the last stronghold of that Berber speech which seems at one time to have prevailed throughout North Africa. Combined with influences from Muslim Spain this has given civilization in Morocco a colouring which it does not have in the east. It is the more noticeable because the country was never subject to the Turkish influence which so profoundly affected the rest of the Arab world.

Morocco has inherited from the two centuries when the authority of its rulers extended from the Sahara to northern Portugal and Catalonia, and from the Atlantic to the Gulf of Gabes, an imperial outlook and air which it at no time entirely lost. Even in the deca-dence of the nineteenth century, Europeans called the country the Sherifian Empire, and Lord Palmerston used to style the ruler 'Emperor'. Throughout the centuries the Moroccan Sultans con-trolled the trade routes to West Africa through Mauritania and through Tuat and the Central Sahara. The local notables who administered the latter areas, in so far as any administration existed, sought confirmation of their position from the Sultan and looked to him for aid in time of trouble. It was only in 1902 that France put an end to this connexion and it was as recently as 1934 that she com-pleted the conquest of Morocco by sending an expedition south through Tinduf to Mauritania where it joined up with other French forces coming from the south. The subsequent transfer of some of these latter territories to Algeria, for reasons of purely French interest, and the making of Mauritania into an independent state, have left a sense of grievance, common to all politically, minded Moroccans, which does not diminish. In 1958 when the Provisional Government of the Algerian Republic was formed Morocco gave full support to its claim against the French for inde, pendence within the existing Algerian frontiers, but made the proviso that she reserved her own claim for settlement in discussions with the future independent Algerian government. When the successor of the provisional Algerian government, which accepted aid on these terms, was reluctant to open negotiations, much friction and a number of frontier incidents ensued. These culminated in an outbreak of hostilities in October 1963 when Algerian forces, making a surprise attack, killed a number of Moroccan homeguards who were occupying a desert water hole which French maps appar, ently showed as Moroccan but which the Algerian government believed to be on their side of the frontier. Moroccan forces then re, captured the position and repelled further Algerian attacks, including an assault on the undoubtedly Moroccan town of Figuig. A cease fire, arranged by the mediation of the Emperor of Ethiopia, was later confirmed by the Organization for African Unity to which the dispute was referred. But the original issue remains unsolved.

Morocco stands in a special relationship to Spain. In a certain sense the countries are twins. Each lies at the far end of the cultural unit to which it belongs, Morocco at the extremity of the Arab world, Spain at the extremity of western Europe. Together they form an intermediate area between the European and the Semitic home, lands, having some of the geographical characteristics of both. The French witticism that Africa begins at the Pyrenees yields its full meaning only when we add that Europe begins at the Atlas. A powerful régime in Morocco tends to regard Spain as a natural prolongation of itself to the north. The Almohad Caliph to whom King John sent an embassy used to refer to Spain as the 'second Maghrib'. A powerful régime north of the Straits tends in the same way to regard Morocco as a natural extension of itself to the south. From the dawn of history reciprocal influences have been common,

Economic map of Morocco

and from the moment when the Arabs invaded Spain from Morocco until the seventeenth century a constant current of Andalusian Arab influence flowed south across the Straits. These links were strengthened by the two hundred years of Moroccan rule in Spain, and the word 'Moorish' came to be used to describe a civilization common to both areas. During the recent protectorate, a Spanish official declared that his country looked forward to 'the restoration of a free and great Moroccan people, united with Spain in the closest brotherhood . . . a people who will collaborate with her in a magnificent revival of Hispano-Arabic culture'.[35] The difficulty of such collaboration is that Hispano-Arab culture is inextricably involved with Islam while Hispano-Latin culture is equally bound up with Christianity. Though religion no longer dominates the life of either people to the same extent as it once did, it is hard to imagine a Hispano-Arabic culture which was not so definitely Islamic as to be unacceptable to Christian Spaniards. Though Ceuta and Melilla have been enclaves in Moroccan territory for over 400 years, and their population is almost entirely Spanish, their existence is a Moroccan grievance just as the British occupation of Gibraltar is a Spanish grievance. The far more recently occupied Ifni is a more acute irritant. Probably Spain would agree to surrender the latter in return for guarantees from the Moroccan government about the former, but so far there have been few signs of any such guarantees being given. Apart from these questions of frontier adjustment, Morocco has no foreign ambitions and is not in the least likely to embark on an ambitious foreign policy like that of the UAR nor to indulge in quixotic sallies on behalf of distressed peoples such as appeal to President Benbella. But she would of course have decided views about her own status in a more closely united Maghrib.

France's special position in Morocco, unlike that of Spain, is due not to natural affinity and geographical proximity but to the continuing strength of the French connexion built up during the protectorate. Most educated Moroccans understand French and are familiar with French ways of thought and French methods. On the other hand the native institutions of the country and its traditions were not destroyed by conquest during the forty years protectorate,

as they were in neighbouring Algeria, or as the result of an annexation which lasted for a century and a quarter. The mass of Moroccans
never became an under-employed proletariat as the majority of
Algerians did, nor was independence preceded in their case by
eight years of desperate struggle. Even in Algeria it was the sudden
disappearance of nine-tenths of the French population as much as
free choice which decided the government to entrust the agreement
of the former European-controlled industries and farms to committees
of Muslim Algerian workers. In Morocco where no such pressure
existed not only are the schools largely manned by French teachers
(as in the case in Algeria itself) but industry too is still mainly
owned and managed by Frenchmen, who often depend on Spaniards and Portuguese to provide the foremen and skilled workers.
Unlike Algeria, and even Tunisia, seven years passed in Morocco
before plans were made to take over even the first fifth of the quarter
million hectares of European-owned farms which provide 60 per
cent of Morocco's agricultural exports. While Moroccan students
are highly susceptible to revolutionary pressure from other Arab
lands and from elsewhere, it is doubtful whether such pressure
exerts a dominant influence outside certain limited and mainly
urban areas. The strong individuality of Morocco will no doubt
increasingly assert itself in one way after another but it seems equally
certain that French influence must remain important for at least
several more decades.

In home affairs the major issue is that of the régime. Though the
promulgation of the constitution marked a great advance, it left
ultimate authority with the King. The system of government is
authoritarian, having certain parallels with the Gaullist system
which may in part have inspired it. It continues, as King Hassan II
has expressed it, 'a fourteen-century-old dialogue between Moroccan
sovereigns and their people'. There is a parliament; political parties
are able to exist and to propagate their views with great freedom. A
greater degree of political freedom is to be found today in Morocco
than in any other Muslim Arab State because of the monarchy's existence. When General Juin in 1951 demanded that Mohammed V
should disassociate himself from the Istiqlal Party, the Sultan based

his refusal on the claim that the monarchy was above parties and that the issue therefore did not arise. This may have been taken at the time as a mere excuse, but it probably represented the Sultan's profound conviction. After independence it was not difficult for him to prevent the Istiqlal from establishing one-party rule. His prestige was enormous, while the Istiqlal on the other hand incurred widespread resentment on account of the high proportion of posts which it secured for its members. One result of this was the formation in October 1957 of a new group, the *Mouvement Populaire*, animated principally by distrust of the Istiqlal and having its chief support in rural, mainly Berber, areas. It was led by Mahjoub Ahardan, who had to leave his post as governor of Rabat district, and by the former Liberation Army organizer, Dr Abdelkrim Khatib.

It soon became clear that there was also a deep division of opinion within the ranks of the Istiqlal itself. The link between its members had been the will to independence rather than a common doctrine in internal affairs or universal devotion to a leader. The party president, Allal al-Fasi, was as much scholar and thinker as he was political leader; the Secretary General, Ahmed Balafrej, seemed cast for the role of senior statesman rather than that of party organizer. The leaders who controlled the party machinery could be described as Islamic conservatives; they were perfectly content to support, and participate in, coalition governments provided that the party was allotted a sufficient number of suitable ministries. They had little sympathy with the colleagues who wanted much quicker constitutional advance, and who – though they did not say so – probably looked on republicanism with no unfavourable eye. Failing to get satisfaction, the 'progressives' broke away in 1959 and after trying in vain to sustain their claim to be the true champions of Istiqlal principles formed a party of their own, the *Union Nationale des Forces Populaires* (UNFP). They demanded that the promised constitution should be drafted by an elected assembly; and that in the meanwhile there should be a clear definition of the powers and responsibilities of ministers. They should not be departmental heads, individually responsible to the King, but a body which possessed constitutional and collective responsibility for the formulation and execution of policy. Since the King had already rejected this suggestion, with some asperity, before the split, they refused to participate in any government that he formed. In 1960 this attitude led Mohammed V to assume the position of Prime Minister himself, pending the promulgation of a Constitution which was promised for the end of 1962, and to announce his intention of chosing his ministers henceforth only for their 'loyalty, integrity, and ability' and not on considerations of party strength. In spring 1963, the first elections were held for the lower house. These gave the government a number of seats only just about equal to those won by the two opposition parties. In July, shortly before the elections were due for the local councils which would determine the composition of the second house, a number of UNFP members were arrested, and later tried, and eleven of them condemned, on a charge of plotting to assassinate the King and forcibly to overthrow the régime. Attempts of this nature have been too common in the Afro-Asian world, and too often condoned by success, for the alleged occurrence of such a conspiracy to appear surprising, even though there was no justification in Morocco for resort to such methods. But government credit suffered, in France as well as in Morocco, from the conduct of the police in apparently employing torture to extort evidence and from the prosecution's handling of the trial; this was, however, public and full. It seems most unlikely that an attempt to subvert the régime by such means could have succeeded, though it might have done great damage before being suppressed. The prestige of the monarchy is still great; the country districts certainly would not prefer the rule of a political party to that of the King. Hassan II, equally at home in French and Arabic, is a hard-working ruler who gives the impression of being perhaps the ablest and most responsible statesman in the country. His disappearance would be an irreplaceable loss since his heir is an infant in arms, and a regency would be no substitute for a resolute ruler. However the mere occurrence of an abortive conspiracy would in itself have had little significance if the UNFP of which the accused were adherents had not been such an influential body. Among them was the Secretary General of the Party, Mehdi

ben Barka, formerly President of the National Consultative
Assembly, well known abroad as one of the most alert and modern
minded of Moroccans. During the struggle for independence the
French had nicknamed him their 'enemy number one'. Happening
to be out of the country at the time of the arrests, he was sentenced to
death *in absentia* for treasonable utterance during the fighting on the
Algerian frontier and again later for alleged participation in the plot.
Other leaders of the party (not accused of complicity) included
Abdurrahim Bouabid, first Moroccan Ambassador to France and
later Minister of National Economy and Vice-Premier.

In Morocco moreover the UNFP appeals strongly to the most
vocal and politically active among Moroccan students and enjoys
the sympathy of the UMT. Abroad it has close connexions with
ruling circles in Algeria and the UAR and with the French left. In
the industrial areas and coastal towns it has considerable voting
strength; while the Istiqlal dominate in Fez and other traditional
centres, and the government party, the Front for the Defence of
Constitutional Institutions (FDIC) is strongest in the mountains
and pre-Saharan areas. The latter party had been formed in March
1963 by Ahmed Reda Guedira, Director of the Royal Cabinet and
Minister of the Interior and Agriculture, to provide a government
majority in the forthcoming parliament. It included the *Mouvement
Populaire* of Ahardan, now Minister of Defence, but in April 1964
a distinction was made by the formation by Guedira with other
governmental elements of a fresh grouping which was named the
Democratic Socialist Party (PDS). The elections of 1963 for the
lower house of parliament, based on universal suffrage, may have
been somewhat weighted in favour of the government, but the result
may be taken as giving a fair idea of the state of public opinion. The
UNFP gained twenty-eight seats, the Istiqlal forty, and the FDIC
sixty-nine. The UNFP are therefore very definitely a minority.

In the fighting in October 1963 the Moroccan army showed itself
very well able to deal with Algerian attacks, while the violent radio
propaganda directed against the Moroccan régime from Algiers and
Cairo proved singularly ineffective. Clearly the Moroccan government is not going to collapse at the first blast of enemy trumpets. The

country has a favourable geographical position; its considerable natural resources are capable of much further development. The present need is not a revolution, but a greater sense of urgency in government, more technical skill, more application among the rank and file of officials, and a wider spread of education. All things considered, Morocco has a better chance than many new states of achieving a satisfactory future without first undergoing a violent upheaval or submitting to a one-party dictatorship. From the point of view of western democracy it deserves more sympathy than it receives.

Notes on the text

3 THE ALMORAVID EMPIRE

1 Summarized from Ibn Said in *Nafh al-Tib* by al-Maqqari (Gayango's translation, vol. 1), London, 1840, p. 118.

2 Ibn Rashiq, quoted in *Kitab al-Muajib fi Talkhis Akhbar al-Maghrib*, ed. P. Dozy, 1847, p. 50.

3 Ibn Alcama in the *Primera Cronica General*. See M. Pidal, *La España del Cid*, Madrid, 1929, vol. II, p. 522.

4 *Kitab al-Muajib*, as above, pp. 122 and 128.

4 THE ALMOHAD CALIPHATE AND THE BENI MARIN

5 E. Lévi-Provençal, *Documents Inédits d'Histoire Almohade*, Memoirs of al-Baidaq, Paris, 1928.

6 *Kitab al-Muajib*, as above, p. 151.

7 Ibn Marzuq, ed. E. Lévi-Provençal, *Al-Musnad*, pp. 38, 39.

5 COLLAPSE AND RECOVERY

8 A. Herculano, *Portugaliae monumenta historica (Scriptores)*, Lisbon, 1856, p. 398.

9 P. de Cenival (trans.), *Chronique de Santa Cruz de Cabo de Gué* (Agadir), Paris, 1934, p. 53.

10 *Nuzhat al-Hadi*, Fez, 1370 (1889–90), p. 47.

11 G. Peele, *Battle of Alcazar*, Marlowe Society Reprint, 1907, lines 1080 et seq.

12 Ed. and trans. O. Houdas, *Tedzkiret en-Nisian*, Paris, 1901, p. IX.

13 *Nuzhat al-Hadi*, as above, p. 82.

14 *Nuzhat al-Hadi*, as above, pp. 86, 87.

6 COLLAPSE AND WITHDRAWAL

15 T. Zammit, *History of Malta*, Valetta, 1929, p. 248.

16 A. Dobson (ed.), *The Diary of John Evelyn*, London, 1906, vol. I, pp. 124, 125.

17 R. Brown (ed.), *The Adventures of T. Pellow*, by himself, London, 1890, pp. 57, 58.

18 Ahmad al-Nasiri al-Salawi, *Kitab al-Istiqsa* (French trans.), *Archives Marocaines*, vol. IX, Paris, 1906, p. 132.

19 M. Castellanos, *Historia de Marruecos*, Tangier, 1898, p. 452.

20 Abu al-Qasim al-Zayyani, *Al-Turjuman al-Muarib* (ed. and trans. O. Houdas), Paris, 1886, p. 52.

21 J. Windus, *A Journey to Mequinez*, London, 1725, pp. 101–2.

22 W. B. Harris, *Journey to Tafilet*, London, 1895, pp. 332–3.

23 E. Aubin, *Le Maroc d'aujourd'hui*, Paris, 1904, p. 220.

7 THE SCENE CHANGES
24 P. Loti, *Maroc*, Paris, 1926, p. 357.

25 *Le Maroc d'aujourd'hui*, as above, p. 245.

26 T. Ellwood, *History of his life, narrated by himself*, 3rd ed., London, 1765 (refers to 1662), pp. 159–60.

27 *Journey to Tafilet*, as above, pp. 23–5.

28 *Le Maroc d'aujourd'hui*, as above, pp. 335, 336.

29 G. Mouette, *Visit to Fez* in J. Stevens, *New Collection of Voyages*, vol. II, London, 1711, pp. 14, 15.

30 A. de Larrea Palacín, *Canciones Juglarescas de Ifni*, Madrid, 1956, pp. 228–30.

31 R. Forbes, *El Raisuni*, London, 1924, pp. 151, 155.

32 P. Marty, *Le Maroc de demain*, Paris, 1925, p. 228.

9 MOROCCO TODAY AND TOMORROW
33 N. Barbour (ed.), *A Survey of North West Africa*, 2nd ed., London, 1962, p. 135.

34 L. Justinard, *Notes d'histoire et de litérature berbères*, *Hesperis*, vol. V, Rabat, 1925, pp. 222–38.

35 T. G. Figueras, *Marruecos*, Madrid, 1944, p. 190.

List of Abbreviations

FDIC Front for Defence of Constitutional Institutions
ONI Office Nationale d'Irrigation
ONMR Office Nationale de la Modernisation Rurale
PDS Democratic Socialist Party
UMI Union Marocaine de Travail
UNFP Union Nationale des Forces Populaires

Select Bibliography

The medieval history of Morocco is recorded in Arabic in the writings of numerous Moroccan chroniclers and, up to 1400, in those of the great Tunisian historian of Andalusian origin, Ibn Khaldun. The more important of these works are available in French, and some also in Spanish, translations. Ibn Khaldun's famous introductory chapters, known as *al-Muqaddimah*, are available also in the English translation of F. Rosenthal (London, 1958). A Moroccan writer, al-Nasiri al-Salawi (1834–97), compiled a history of Morocco, *Kitab al-Istiqsa*, from earliest times till 1894 (Cairo, 1897). A French translation is available in *Archives Marocaines*, vols. IX (1906) and X (1907). Details of these and of European works are to be found in the bibliographies in Charles-André Julien's *Histoire de l'Afrique du Nord*, vol. II (revised edition, Paris, 1961), and Henri Terrasse's *Histoire du Maroc* (Casablanca, 1949–50); these two works contain the most complete and scholarly treatment of their respective subjects, though in the case of the latter allowance must be made for the author's bias.

From the Saadian period onwards an immense number of documents in English, French, Spanish, Portuguese, Dutch, and Arabic, mostly from European record offices, accompanied by introductions and French summaries, have been made available in the *Les Sources Inédites de l'Histoire du Maroc* (Paris, 1901), edited by the Comte de Castries. For Maulay Ismail's reign, *A Journey to Mequinez* in 1721 by J. Windus, of Commodore Stewart's embassy (London, 1725); *The Adventures of T. Pellow* by the English captive and renegade, Thomas Pellow (ed. R. Brown, London, 1890); and the English translation of the books of the French captive G. Mouette in Steven's *New Collection of Voyages*, vol. II (London, 1711), are all to be recommended. For the anarchic period following Maulay Ismail's death, there is an interesting account by Captain Braithwaite, *History of the Revolutions in Morocco* (London, 1729); and (in a French translation) the account of the captivity of the very remarkable Dutch woman, Maria Ter Meetelen, oddly entitled *L'Annotation*

Ponctuelle (Paris, 1956). Dr William Lemprières, *A Tour of Morocco* (London, 1791), is informative about the Tarudant area at the end of the eighteenth century. A hundred years later the books of Budgett Meakin, whose *Moorish Empire* (London, 1899) gives most of the sources of Moroccan history known at that date, are valuable. F. R. Fleurnoy's *British Policy towards Morocco 1830–1865* (Baltimore, 1935) admirably covers the subjects indicated. There is an English translation of Eugène Aubin's excellent account of Morocco in 1903, with the title *Morocco Today* (London, 1904). The works of Walter B. Harris cover the period from 1894 to 1912, and he is the author also of *France, Spain and the Rif* (London, 1927). Raisuni's life is vividly recorded, largely in his own words, in *El Raisuni* by Rosita Forbes (London, 1924).

Since that date books in English showing an intimate knowledge of the Moroccan scene have been few and far between. Of several works by Rom Landau, *Moroccan Drama 1900–1955* (London, 1956) gives a serviceable journa⸗listic account of the period. Nina Epton's *Under the Crescent Moon* (London, 1949) and Marvine Howe's *One Woman's Morocco* (London, 1955) give interesting glimpses of Moroccan and French points of view at the periods concerned. Douglas Ashford's *Political Change in Morocco* (Princeton, 1961) gives a mass of accurate fact about the Istiqlal Party shortly after independence, but is a book for the specialist. *A Survey of North West Africa* edited by N. Barbour (2nd ed., London, 1962), devotes 140 pages to Morocco, dealing principally with contemporary political and economic issues. *Planning in Morocco* by A. Waterston (London, 1962) is a serious study of the effort to formulate a ten⸗year plan. Charles Gallagher's *The United States and North Africa* (New York, 1963) has an illuminating section on Morocco.

The history of the nationalist movement in Morocco up to 1947 is included in Allal al⸗Fasi's *The Independence Movements in Arab North Africa* (Washington, 1954, from an Arabic original published in Cairo in 1948). Information on this subject is also given in Mehdi A. Bennouna's *Our Morocco* (Morocco, 1951).

In French there is a vast literature on Morocco (apart from the former northern zone). The best general accounts of modern Morocco are *Le Maroc à l'Epreuve* of Jean and Simone Lacouture (Paris, 1958) and *Maroc* (Paris, 1962) by Vincent Monteil. Political development is well covered in André Julien's *L'Afrique du Nord en marche* (Paris, 1952); and in Roger Le Tourneau's *Évolution Politique de l'Afrique du Nord Musulmane 1920–1961* (Paris, 1962), which also lists other works. On sociological aspects of Morocco the writings of Robert Montagne, Jacques Berque, and André Adam are outstanding; on art, those of Henri Terrasse.

In Spanish there are valuable translations of medieval Moroccan historians, and studies of Almohad history, by Ambrosio Huici Miranda; while the Almoravid period is covered in *Los Almoravides* by J. Bosch-Vila (Tetuan, 1956). For administration in the Spanish zone the works of Tomas García Figueras may be consulted; on the Spanish Sahara, those of Caro Baroja and Hernandez Pacheco; on life as a prisoner of the Rogui (Bu Hamara) *Tres Sultanes a la Porfía de un Reino* by Enrique Arques (Tetuan, 1953).

The authority on the Portuguese in Morocco is David Lopes in *Historia de Portugal, edicão monumental*, vol. III (Barcelos, 1931), Ch. 3 & 4 and vol. IV (1932), Ch. 2.

Finally a few books written by Moroccans in French deserve mention. Mohammed Lahbabi is author of a brilliant study of the position of the Moroccan monarchy before the protectorate entitled *Le Gouvernement Marocain à l'aube du XXème siècle* (Rabat, 1958). *Le Boîte à Merveilles* by Ahmed Sefrioui (Paris, 1954) is a charming story of an old-world childhood in Fez. *Le Passé Simple* by Driss Chraibi (Paris, 1954) presents a terrifying picture of Muslim family relationships in the transition period. *L'Oreille en écharpe* (Casablanca, undated) by Ahmed Belhachmi gives a picture of religious hypocrisy in the head of a family, in the form of a comedy with acid undertones.

Innumerable aspects of Moroccan history, art, archaeology, and sociology are treated in the publications of the former *École des Hautes Études Marocaines* at Rabat (now part of the University of Rabat) and in those of the Instituto Maulay Hassan of Tetuan. There is now a combined publication, *Hesperis-Tamuda*.

Who's Who

AHARDAN, Mahjoub, b. 1921. Passed out of Military Academy in Meknès. Served with Moroccan troops in French Army; mentioned in despatches of World War II. Caid of Oulmes 1949–53 until dismissed for pro-nationalist activities. Commander in Moroccan Liberation Army 1954–5. Governor of Rabat area till dismissed for political activities in connexion with the founding of the Popular Movement in 1958. Minister of Defence, 1961.

BAHNINI, Ahmed, b. 1909. Studied law and served as interpreter for ten years. Member of Fez Bar in 1942. Was first President of Moroccan Supreme Court after independence, and then Secretary General of the Ministry of the Interior. Minister of Justice in January 1963. Appointed Premier on 13 November 1963 immediately before opening of first Moroccan Parliament.

BALAFREJ, Hajj Ahmed, b. 1908. Educated College of Sons of Notables and Lycée Gouraud, Rabat. Later attended Cairo University and the Sorbonne. *Licence ès Lettres* and *Diplôme des Hautes Etudes de la Sorbonne*. Secretary General, Istiqlal Party, 1943. Imprisoned 1944. After independence first Foreign Minister, April 1956 till May 1958. Premier and Foreign Minister, May 1958 till December 1958. In March 1961 appointed Personal Representative of King Hassan and from December 1961 Foreign Minister until November 1963 when he retained only the former post.

BARKA, Mehdi ben, b. 1920. Took leading part in nationalist movement and described by French as 'Enemy Number One'. President of National Consultative Assembly 1956 till its dissolution in 1959. In 1959 seceded from Istiqlal and formed National Union of Popular Forces. From 1960 lived abroad in self-imposed exile for two years. Attacked Moroccan régime from Cairo during Moroccan Algerian frontier fighting in autumn 1963 and was condemned to death *in absentia* by a special court.

BATUTA, Ibn, 1304–78. Most famous of Muslim travellers. Travelled in the Middle East, Central Asia, India, China, Central Africa, and Spain. At the order of Sultan Abu Inan he dictated an account of his travels in Fez in 1355.

BEKKAI, Embarak, Si (1907–61). First Moroccan Prime Minister after indepen‑ dence. Of Berber origin, he entered the Dar al‑Baida military academy at Meknès and fought with distinction in World War II in France, losing a leg and attaining the rank of Colonel. As Pasha of Sefrou in 1953 he resigned in protest against the deportation of the Sultan. Prime Minister from 1955 to 1956, he headed a reformed administration from the latter year until 1958. From 1960 he was Minister of the Interior until his death.

BOUABID, Abdurrahim, b. 1920. Family of modest means. Editor of the Istiqlal paper *al‑Alam* during nationalist struggle. Minister of State in first Independent Government, 1955. Ambassador in Paris, 1956. Minister of Economy, 1956. Vice‑Premier and Minister of Economy, 1958 till 1960. Since then active opposition leader in UNFP.

FASI, Mohammed Allal al‑, b. 1906. Educated Qarawiyin University. Active in nationalist movement from 1926. Exiled to Gabon in 1937 where he learned French and extended his education by reading during the nine years till he was released in 1946. President of Istiqlal Party. Forbidden to return to Fez before independence, lived in Tangier, Cairo, and Spain. Refused ministerial office until creation of Ministry of Islamic Affairs in 1961. Resigned in 1963, when Istiqlal Party went into opposition. Author of *The Independence Movements in Arab North Africa* and of *Auto‑Critique*, both in Arabic (English translation of former, Washington, 1954). Leading advocate of the Greater Morocco on which he has published many articles.

GLAWI, Thami al‑ (1886–1956). Berber chief in High Atlas and Pasha of Marrakesh. His brother, Madani al‑Glawi, was Grand Vizir to Maulay Abd al‑Hafidh. After Madani's death, Thami supported French in High Atlas area in early days of protectorate and was rewarded by retention and great enlargement of his semi‑independent fief there. From 1950 headed French‑ encouraged resistance of certain traditional elements against the nationalist movement. In 1951 was dismissed from the Palace for telling Mohammed V that he was Sultan of the Istiqlal Party, not of Morocco. Highly praised by French authorities he headed movement against Sultan in 1953, but humbly submitted to him in 1955, dying some months later.

GUEDIRA, Ahmed Reda, b. 1922. Educated at College for the Sons of Notables and Lycée Gouraud at Rabat. Law degree in Paris. Minister of State, 1955. Minister of Information and Tourism 1956 until 1958. Director of Cabinet of Crown Prince Maulay Hassan, 1960. Director of Royal Cabinet, 1961. Minister of Interior and Agriculture in 1961, and delegate entitled to exercise certain prerogatives of Premier on behalf of King Hassan. In March 1963 organized Front for the Defence of Constitutional Liberties to support Royal Government. Foreign Minister, November 1963. Director of the weekly *Les Phares* which expressed the point of view of the Palace.

HAFIDH, Maulay Abd al- (dates unknown), last Sultan of pre-protectorate Morocco. While Lord Lieutenant of his brother, Sultan Abd al-Aziz, in Marrakesh in 1908, he declared the latter deposed as having betrayed the country to the infidel, raised troops, and marched north. Having defeated his brother's forces and made an abortive attack on the French troops occupying the area south of Casablanca was proclaimed Sultan in Fez, where he took up residence. Forced by increasing anarchy to seek French protection, he had no choice but to sign the Treaty of Fez in March 1912. Subsequently abdicated, living as a pensioner in Tangier till his death.

HASSAN, Abu al- (1330-51). Greatest of the Merinid Sultans. Last Moroccan sovereign to compaign in the eastern Maghrib, and in Spain. Built the necro-polis of Chella outside Rabat.

HASSAN II, b. 1928. King of Morocco. Eldest son of Mohammed V. Educated at the College for the Sons of Notables in Rabat, he took a degree in law at Bordeaux University. Succeeded on death of his father on 26 February 1961. Confidant and adviser of his father during the struggle for independence and after independence. He accompanied his father in exile, 1953-5. Appointed Chief of Staff, 1956. Invested as Crown Prince, 1957. Vice-Premier in 1960 when his father assumed the Premiership. On succeeding to the throne, he retained the office of Premier until after the elections for the first Parliament in November 1963.

IBRAHIM, Maulay Abdullah, b. 1918. Educated Madrasa ben Yusuf. Secretary of State for Information, 1955. Minister of Labour and Social Questions, 1956. Prime Minister and Minister of Foreign Affairs, 1958, until dismissed by King in 1960. For long a figure in UNFP, he has since been more closely connected with the UMT. Author of *Le Maroc au Travail*, 1957.

IDRIS I. Great-grandson of Prophet Muhammad. Escaped from Arabia when his family was proscribed and reached Walili (Volubilis) with the help of a faithful retainer. In 788 was chosen as ruler by local Berbers of Auruba tribe and campaigned to reduce local non-Muslims to submission. Died 791.

IDRIS II. Posthumous son of above by Berber mother. Founded new city at Fez which he made his capital. Welcomed further groups of Arab refugees from the east who formed his advisers and bodyguard. Made Fez a centre of Arab and Islamic influence and he is regarded as the founder of the Moroccan state. Died 822. In 1437 the supposed discovery of his incorrupted body at a shrine in Fez gave an impulse to his cult in Fez which is still important today.

ISMAIL, Maulay (1672–1727). Alawite ruler of immense energy and vitality. Made Meknès his capital and endowed it with vast buildings. Reputed very cruel, he displayed occasional kindnesses also. Famous for the number of his children. He created an army of black slaves who were systematically bred and brought up. Carried on a correspondence with Louis XIV and James II.

JUIN, General, later Marshal, Alphonse (b. *circa* 1890). Distinguished French soldier of Algerian settler origin. Commanded Free French troops in Italy during World War II. In 1947 he was appointed Resident General in Morocco to combat nationalism and with authority to take what measures he thought necessary to deal with Sultan Mohammed V's opposition. Resorting to increasingly strong measures he extorted a partial submission from the Sultan in 1951, after tribal demonstrations of which he was suspected of being the inspirer. His transfer to a high military post some months later was widely believed to be a courteous disavowal of his methods by the French government.

KHATTABI, Mohammed Abdelkrim al- (Abd al-Karim) (1882–1963). Son of the Caid of the Beni Ouriaghel, a Berber tribe situated near Alhucemas. Worked with the Spanish in Native Affairs Department at Melilla. Edited *El Telegramma del Rif* and was Chief Cadi of Melilla area. After being imprisoned by the Spaniards took arms against them and inflicted a disaster on a Spanish army at Anual in 1921. He then created the 'Republic of the Rif', but was defeated by overwhelming French and Spanish forces in 1926 and exiled to Reunion. Allowed to sail from France in 1947, he left the ship at Port Said and took refuge in Egypt, where he died in 1963.

LYAUTEY, General, later Marshal, Louis Hubert Gonsalve (1854–1934), first and most distinguished French Resident General in Morocco. Appointed in April 1912, he showed much sympathy with Moroccan tradition and was responsible for the particular style given to the protectorate. In 1914 when ordered to withdraw to coast to free troops for the front in France managed to retain all occupied territory while sending more troops than requested. After being War Minister in France for three months in 1917 returned to Morocco till resignation in 1925. Organized administration reducing resistance in tribal areas of Atlas and halting Adbelkrim's onslaught in 1925. Was buried in Moorish-style monument in Rabat, but his remains were transferred to France when Morocco received independence.

MANSUR, Ahmad al- (1578–1603). Greatest of the Saadian Sultans. Spent some years in exile in Constantinople with his mother and his brother, Abd al-Malik. Succeeded after the death of the latter, at the Battle of Alcazarquivir. Carried on active diplomatic relations with Queen Elizabeth, encouraging trade between Morocco and England and hoping to form an alliance to fight Spain. Sent an expedition across the Sahara in 1591 which conquered the black empire of Songhai and established a Moroccan protectorate with its capital in Timbuctu.

MOHAMMED V (1927–61). Third son of Maulay Yusuf, he was born in 1911 and succeeded his father in 1927. After World War II he took an outstanding role in securing independence from the French. Deposed in 1953 and deported to Madagascar, he made a triumphal re-entry in 1955. In 1957 he assumed the title of King. Died unexpectedly of heart failure after a minor operation in 1961.

MUMIN, Abd al- (1129–62). Disciple and successor of Ibn Tumart and first Almohad Caliph. Great soldier and administrator, extended Almohad rule over all North Africa to Tripolitania and over Muslim Spain.

NAFI, Uqba ibn, b. *circa* 630. Arab general. Nephew of Amr ibn al-As the conqueror of Egypt, he was appointed to command in Ifriqiya (Tunisia) in 663, and founded Kairawan in 670. Five years later a new governor of Egypt replaced him by another commander who took Arab arms as far as Algiers and possibly Tlemsen. Having complained to the Caliph at Damascus, Uqba was reappointed by him in 682. During his second governorship he made his famous raid as far as the Atlantic shore, south of the Atlas. On the return journey, having over-confidently broken up his army, he was ambushed in south-east Algeria, where his tomb is still to be seen in the oasis called after him, about twelve miles from Biskra.

RAISUNI, Ahmad al- (The Sherif), b. *circa* 1870. In his twenties took to a Robin Hood style of life in the hills and was imprisoned in Mogador by Maulay al-Hassan I for five years. He resumed his misconduct on release, but was made Governor of the area outside Tangier by Sultan Abd al-Aziz in hopes of converting his undoubted talents to lawful uses. Complaints about his cruelty led to his dismissal and renewed banditry, in the course of which he kidnapped the Sultan's military adviser, the Scot, Caid Sir Harry Maclean, for whom he secured a ransom of £20,000. In 1908 sided with Maulay Abd al-Hafidh and was appointed Governor of Arzila, where he at times assisted and at times resisted the Spanish infiltration. Finally, having engaged in open war, he was besieged by them in his mountain refuge, but was captured by Adbelkrim and transported to the Rif, where he died shortly afterwards. A man of personality and charm, in spite of his misdeeds. He dictated his life to Rosita Forbes in 1923.

SEDDIQ, Mahjoub ben, b. 1922. Secretary General, *Union Marocain de Travail*. Close to UNFP. Formerly stationmaster on Moroccan railways. Vice-President of National Consultative Assembly, 1957. Member of the administrative commission of the African Peoples' Congress and President of AAFTU.

TASHFIN, Yusuf, Ibn (1061–1107). Founder of Almoravid Empire. Created united kingdom, stretching to Algiers in the east and to Catalonia in the north. As ally of the Muslim King of Seville won a great victory over Alfonso VI at Zallaqa (Sagrajas) near Badajoz. Later he dispossessed the Muslim princes of Spain and imposed Almoravid rule. Member of Sanhaja branch of veiled Berber nomads from Mauritania. Extremely devout and of very simple manner of life.

TUMART, Muhammad, Ibn (b. *circa* 1080–1130). Religious reformer and revolutionary leader. Learned Theologian. Travelled to the east in search of religious knowledge in 1107 and returned to Marrakesh in 1121. Expelled from the capital, he organized a fighting religious community out of the Masmouda Berbers in the High Atlas at Tinmel, forming the Almohad community. Believed by his followers to be the Mahdi, exempt from sin.

Acknowledgements

For permission to reproduce photographs:

Archives Photographiques, 59; Associated Press, 63; by courtesy of the Trustees of the British Museum, 20, 21, 37; Camera Press, 57, 77, 90; from H. de Castries, *Les Sources inédite de l'histoire du Maroc de 1530 à 1845*, 1905, by courtesy of the Trustees of the British Museum, 45; Éditions du Seuil, 50, 52, 54; O. Ford, 6, 71; from J. Graberg *Specchio geografico e statistico dell'Impero di Marocco*, 1834, by courtesy of the Trustees of the British Museum, 3; *Illustrated London News*, 61; S. Kostomaroff, 16; Keystone Press Agency, 68, 69, 72, 73, 74, 75, 76, 79; by kind permission of the Moroccan ambassador, Prince Hassan ben el Mehdi, 43, 44, 46, 51, 61, 64; by courtesy of the Museum of Antiquities, Rabat, 17, 18; from S. Ockley *An Account of S. W. Barbary*, 1713, by courtesy of the Trustees of the British Museum, 48; by courtesy of *Office National Marocain du Tourisme*, 4, 5, 7, 8, 14, 15, 18, 19, 23, 24, 25, 26, 29, 30, 35, 36, 39, 40, 41, 47, 49, 53, 85, 86, 88; Pottecher, 78; Radio Times Hulton Picture Library, 2, 10, 11, 12, 22, 55, 58, 66, 67; B. Rouget, 80, 81, 91; Spanish National Tourist Office, 31, 33, 34; Studios du Souissi, 28, 38, 82, 83, 84, 87; R. Viollet, 42, 56, 62, 65, 70, 89; E. Wilford, 1, 9, 13, 27, 32.

For permission to cite from published works:

E. Aubin, *Le Maroc d'aujourd'hui*, Librairie Armand Colin, Paris, 1904, on pp 128, 144–5, 151; N. Barbour (ed.), *A Survey of North West Africa*, 2nd ed., Oxford University Press, London, 1961, on p 206; P. Loti, *Au Maroc*, Calmann-Lévy, Paris, 1926 on p 141; L. Palacín, *Canciones Juglarescas de Ifni*, Instituto de Estudios Africanos, Madrid, 1956, on p 150.

Index

Numbers in italics refer to illustrations